Early Years Foundation Stage

Statutory Framework,
Outcomes & Development Matters

To purchase a copy please visit:

www.thenationalcurriculum.com

or scan this code to take you there:

Corporate Author (Framework & Outcomes): The Department For Education
Corporate Author (Development Matters): Early Education

Published by: Shurville Publishing

The documents in this book are also available to download from: www.education.gov.uk

The Bournemouth & Poole College

250249597 0

Contents

Statutory Framework for the Early Years Foundation Stage

Setting the standards for learning, development and care for children from birth to five

Published March 2014

Effective September 2014

Summary

About this statutory framework

This framework is mandatory for all early years providers (from 1 September 2014)[1]: maintained schools; non-maintained schools; independent schools; all providers on the Early Years Register; and all providers registered with an early years childminder agency[2].

Ofsted and inspectorates of independent schools have regard to the Early Years Foundation Stage (EYFS) in carrying out inspections and report on the quality and standards of provision. Ofsted publishes inspection reports at *www.ofsted.gov.uk*. Ofsted may issue a *notice to improve* (in respect of any failure to meet a requirement in the document) and/or may issue a *welfare requirements notice* (in respect of Section 3). It is an offence for a provider to fail to comply with a *welfare requirements notice*. Early years childminder agencies are also under a duty to have regard to the EYFS in the exercise of their functions.

Expiry or review date

This statutory framework remains in force until further notice.

What legislation does this framework refer to?

- The learning and development requirements are given legal force by an Order[3] made under section 39(1)(a) of the Childcare Act 2006.

- The safeguarding and welfare requirements are given legal force by Regulations[4] made under section 39(1)(b) of the Childcare Act 2006.

Who is this framework for?

This framework is for all early years providers (from 1 September 2014): maintained schools; non-maintained schools; independent schools; all providers on the Early Years Register; and all providers registered with an early years childminder agency.

.

---

[1] Section 46 of the Childcare Act 2006 enables the Secretary of State to confer exemptions from the learning and development requirements in certain prescribed circumstances.
[2] The Childcare (Exemptions from Registration) Order 2008 (S.I.2008/979) specifies the circumstances in which providers are not required to register.
[3] The Early Years Foundation Stage (Learning and Development Requirements) Order 2007 (S.I. 2007/1772), as amended.
[4] The Early Years Foundation Stage (Welfare Requirements) Regulations 2012 (S.I. 2012/938), as amended.

Introduction

1.   Every child deserves the best possible start in life and the support that enables them to fulfil their potential. Children develop quickly in the early years and a child's experiences between birth and age five have a major impact on their future life chances. A secure, safe and happy childhood is important in its own right. Good parenting and high quality early learning together provide the foundation children need to make the most of their abilities and talents as they grow up.

2.   The Early Years Foundation Stage (EYFS) sets the standards that all early years providers must meet to ensure that children learn and develop well and are kept healthy and safe. It promotes teaching and learning to ensure children's 'school readiness' and gives children the broad range of knowledge and skills that provide the right foundation for good future progress through school and life.

3.   The EYFS seeks to provide:

- **quality and consistency** in all early years settings, so that every child makes good progress and no child gets left behind;

- **a secure foundation** through learning and development opportunities which are planned around the needs and interests of each individual child and are assessed and reviewed regularly;

- **partnership working** between practitioners and with parents and/or carers;

- **equality of opportunity** and anti-discriminatory practice, ensuring that every child is included and supported.

4.   The EYFS specifies requirements for learning and development and for safeguarding children and promoting their welfare. The **learning and development requirements** cover:

- the *areas of learning and development* which must shape activities and experiences (*educational programmes*) for children in all early years settings;

- the *early learning goals* that providers must help children work towards (the knowledge, skills and understanding children should have at the end of the academic year in which they turn five); and

- *assessment arrangements* for measuring progress (and requirements for reporting to parents and/or carers).

5.   The **safeguarding and welfare requirements** cover the steps that providers must take to keep children safe and promote their welfare.

Overarching principles

6.   Four guiding principles should shape practice in early years settings. These are:

- every child is a **unique child**, who is constantly learning and can be resilient, capable, confident and self-assured;

- children learn to be strong and independent through **positive relationships**;

- children learn and develop well in **enabling environments**, in which their experiences respond to their individual needs and there is a strong partnership between practitioners and parents and/or carers; and

- **children develop and learn in different ways and at different rates**. The framework covers the education and care of all children in early years provision, including children with special educational needs and disabilities.

Section 1 – The learning and development requirements

1.1. This section defines what providers[5] must do, working in partnership with parents and/or carers, to promote the learning and development of all children in their care, and to ensure they are ready for school. The learning and development requirements are informed by the best available evidence on how children learn and reflect the broad range of skills, knowledge and attitudes children need as foundations for good future progress. Early years providers must guide the development of children's capabilities with a view to ensuring that children in their care complete the EYFS ready to benefit fully from the opportunities ahead of them.

1.2. The EYFS learning and development requirements comprise:

- the seven areas of learning and development and the educational programmes (described below);

- the early learning goals, which summarise the knowledge, skills and understanding that all young children should have gained by the end of the Reception year; and

- the assessment requirements (when and how practitioners must assess children's achievements, and when and how they should discuss children's progress with parents and/or carers).

The areas of learning and development

1.3. There are seven areas of learning and development that must shape educational programmes in early years settings. All areas of learning and development are important and inter-connected. Three areas are particularly crucial for igniting children's curiosity and enthusiasm for learning, and for building their capacity to learn, form relationships and thrive. These three areas, the prime areas, are:

- communication and language;

- physical development; and

- personal, social and emotional development.

1.4. Providers must also support children in four specific areas, through which the three prime areas are strengthened and applied. The specific areas are:

- literacy;

- mathematics;

---

[5] Excluding providers offering care exclusively before and after school or during the school holidays for children who normally attend Reception (or older) class during the school day – see para 3.40

- understanding the world; and

- expressive arts and design.

1.5. Educational programmes must involve activities and experiences for children, as follows.

- **Communication and language** development involves giving children opportunities to experience a rich language environment; to develop their confidence and skills in expressing themselves; and to speak and listen in a range of situations.

- **Physical development** involves providing opportunities for young children to be active and interactive; and to develop their co-ordination, control, and movement. Children must also be helped to understand the importance of physical activity, and to make healthy choices in relation to food.

- **Personal, social and emotional development** involves helping children to develop a positive sense of themselves, and others; to form positive relationships and develop respect for others; to develop social skills and learn how to manage their feelings; to understand appropriate behaviour in groups; and to have confidence in their own abilities.

- **Literacy** development involves encouraging children to link sounds and letters and to begin to read and write. Children must be given access to a wide range of reading materials (books, poems, and other written materials) to ignite their interest.

- **Mathematics** involves providing children with opportunities to develop and improve their skills in counting, understanding and using numbers, calculating simple addition and subtraction problems; and to describe shapes, spaces, and measures.

- **Understanding the world** involves guiding children to make sense of their physical world and their community through opportunities to explore, observe and find out about people, places, technology and the environment.

- **Expressive arts and design** involves enabling children to explore and play with a wide range of media and materials, as well as providing opportunities and encouragement for sharing their thoughts, ideas and feelings through a variety of activities in art, music, movement, dance, role-play, and design and technology.

1.6. Practitioners must consider the individual needs, interests, and stage of development of each child in their care, and must use this information to plan a challenging and enjoyable experience for each child in all of the areas of learning and development. Practitioners working with the youngest children are expected to focus strongly on the three prime areas, which are the basis for successful learning in the other four specific areas. The three prime areas reflect the key skills and capacities all children need to develop and learn effectively, and become ready for school. It is expected that the balance will shift towards a more equal focus on all areas of learning as children grow in confidence and ability within the three prime areas. But throughout the early years, if a child's progress in any prime area gives cause for concern, practitioners must discuss this with the child's parents and/or carers and agree how to support the child. Practitioners must consider whether a child may have a special educational need or disability which requires specialist support. They should link with, and help families to access, relevant services from other agencies as appropriate.

1.7. For children whose home language is not English, providers must take reasonable steps to provide opportunities for children to develop and use their home language in play and learning, supporting their language development at home. Providers must also ensure that children have sufficient opportunities to learn and reach a good standard in English language during the EYFS: ensuring children are ready to benefit from the opportunities available to them when they begin Year 1. When assessing communication, language and literacy skills, practitioners must assess children's skills in English. If a child does not have a strong grasp of English language, practitioners must explore the child's skills in the home language with parents and/or carers, to establish whether there is cause for concern about language delay.

1.8. Each area of learning and development must be implemented through planned, purposeful play and through a mix of adult-led and child-initiated activity. Play is essential for children's development, building their confidence as they learn to explore, to think about problems, and relate to others. Children learn by leading their own play, and by taking part in play which is guided by adults. There is an ongoing judgement to be made by practitioners about the balance between activities led by children, and activities led or guided by adults. Practitioners must respond to each child's emerging needs and interests, guiding their development through warm, positive interaction. As children grow older, and as their development allows, it is expected that the balance will gradually shift towards more activities led by adults, to help children prepare for more formal learning, ready for Year 1.

1.9. In planning and guiding children's activities, practitioners must reflect on the different ways that children learn and reflect these in their practice. Three characteristics of effective teaching and learning are:

- **playing and exploring** - children investigate and experience things, and 'have a go';

- **active learning** - children concentrate and keep on trying if they encounter difficulties, and enjoy achievements; and

- **creating and thinking critically** - children have and develop their own ideas, make links between ideas, and develop strategies for doing things.

1.10. Each child must be assigned a key person[6] (also a safeguarding and welfare requirement - see paragraph 3.27). Providers must inform parents and/or carers of the name of the key person, and explain their role, when a child starts attending a setting. The key person must help ensure that every child's learning and care is tailored to meet their individual needs. The key person must seek to engage and support parents and/or carers in guiding their child's development at home. They should also help families engage with more specialist support if appropriate.

1.11. A quality learning experience for children requires a quality workforce. A well-qualified, skilled staff strongly increases the potential of any individual setting to deliver the best possible outcomes for children. Requirements in relation to staff qualifications are outlined in Section 3.

1.12. The level of progress children should be expected to have attained by the end of the EYFS is defined by the early learning goals set out below.

The early learning goals

The prime areas

Communication and language

Listening and attention: children listen attentively in a range of situations. They listen to stories, accurately anticipating key events and respond to what they hear with relevant comments, questions or actions. They give their attention to what others say and respond appropriately, while engaged in another activity.

Understanding: children follow instructions involving several ideas or actions. They answer 'how' and 'why' questions about their experiences and in response to stories or events.

Speaking: children express themselves effectively, showing awareness of listeners' needs. They use past, present and future forms accurately when talking about events that have happened or are to happen in the future. They develop their own narratives and explanations by connecting ideas or events.

Physical development

Moving and handling: children show good control and co-ordination in large and small movements. They move confidently in a range of ways, safely negotiating space. They handle equipment and tools effectively, including pencils for writing.

Health and self-care: children know the importance for good health of physical exercise, and a healthy diet, and talk about ways to keep healthy and safe. They manage their own

---

[6] In childminding settings, the key person is the childminder.

basic hygiene and personal needs successfully, including dressing and going to the toilet independently.

Personal, social and emotional development

Self-confidence and self-awareness: children are confident to try new activities, and say why they like some activities more than others. They are confident to speak in a familiar group, will talk about their ideas, and will choose the resources they need for their chosen activities. They say when they do or don't need help.

Managing feelings and behaviour: children talk about how they and others show feelings, talk about their own and others' behaviour, and its consequences, and know that some behaviour is unacceptable. They work as part of a group or class, and understand and follow the rules. They adjust their behaviour to different situations, and take changes of routine in their stride.

Making relationships: children play co-operatively, taking turns with others. They take account of one another's ideas about how to organise their activity. They show sensitivity to others' needs and feelings, and form positive relationships with adults and other children.

The specific areas

Literacy

Reading: children read and understand simple sentences. They use phonic knowledge to decode regular words and read them aloud accurately. They also read some common irregular words. They demonstrate understanding when talking with others about what they have read.

Writing: children use their phonic knowledge to write words in ways which match their spoken sounds. They also write some irregular common words. They write simple sentences which can be read by themselves and others. Some words are spelt correctly and others are phonetically plausible.

Mathematics

Numbers: children count reliably with numbers from 1 to 20, place them in order and say which number is one more or one less than a given number. Using quantities and objects, they add and subtract two single-digit numbers and count on or back to find the answer. They solve problems, including doubling, halving and sharing.

Shape, space and measures: children use everyday language to talk about size, weight, capacity, position, distance, time and money to compare quantities and objects and to solve problems. They recognise, create and describe patterns. They explore characteristics of everyday objects and shapes and use mathematical language to describe them.

Understanding the world

People and communities: children talk about past and present events in their own lives and in the lives of family members. They know that other children don't always enjoy the same things, and are sensitive to this. They know about similarities and differences between themselves and others, and among families, communities and traditions.

The world: children know about similarities and differences in relation to places, objects, materials and living things. They talk about the features of their own immediate environment and how environments might vary from one another. They make observations of animals and plants and explain why some things occur, and talk about changes.

Technology: children recognise that a range of technology is used in places such as homes and schools. They select and use technology for particular purposes.

Expressive arts and design

Exploring and using media and materials: children sing songs, make music and dance, and experiment with ways of changing them. They safely use and explore a variety of materials, tools and techniques, experimenting with colour, design, texture, form and function.

Being imaginative: children use what they have learnt about media and materials in original ways, thinking about uses and purposes. They represent their own ideas, thoughts and feelings through design and technology, art, music, dance, role-play and stories.

Section 2 – Assessment

2.1. Assessment plays an important part in helping parents, carers and practitioners to recognise children's progress, understand their needs, and to plan activities and support. Ongoing assessment (also known as formative assessment) is an integral part of the learning and development process. It involves practitioners observing children to understand their level of achievement, interests and learning styles, and to then shape learning experiences for each child reflecting those observations. In their interactions with children, practitioners should respond to their own day-to-day observations about children's progress and observations that parents and carers share.

2.2. Assessment should not entail prolonged breaks from interaction with children, nor require excessive paperwork. Paperwork should be limited to that which is absolutely necessary to promote children's successful learning and development. Parents and/or carers should be kept up-to-date with their child's progress and development. Practitioners should address any learning and development needs in partnership with parents and/or carers, and any relevant professionals.

Progress check at age two

2.3. When a child is aged between two and three, practitioners must review their progress, and provide parents and/or carers with a short written summary of their child's development in the prime areas. This progress check must identify the child's strengths, and any areas where the child's progress is less than expected. If there are significant emerging concerns, or an identified special educational need or disability, practitioners should develop a targeted plan to support the child's future learning and development involving parents and/or carers and other professionals (for example, the provider's Special Educational Needs Co-ordinator or health professionals) as appropriate.

2.4. Beyond the prime areas, it is for practitioners to decide what the written summary should include, reflecting the development level and needs of the individual child. The summary must highlight: areas in which a child is progressing well; areas in which some additional support might be needed; and focus particularly on any areas where there is a concern that a child may have a developmental delay (which may indicate a special educational need or disability). It must describe the activities and strategies the provider intends to adopt to address any issues or concerns. If a child moves settings between the ages of two and three it is expected that the progress check would usually be undertaken by the setting where the child has spent most time. Practitioners must discuss with parents and/or carers how the summary of development can be used to support learning at home.

2.5. Practitioners should encourage parents and/or carers to share information from the progress check with other relevant professionals, including their health visitor and the staff of any new provision the child may transfer to. Practitioners must agree with parents and/or carers when will be the most useful point to provide a summary. Where possible, the progress check and the Healthy Child Programme health and development review at age two (when health visitors gather information on a child's health and development, allowing them to identify any developmental delay and any particular support from which they think the child/family might benefit) should inform each other and support integrated working. This will allow health and education professionals to identify strengths as well as any developmental delay and provide support from which they think the child/family might benefit. Providers must have the consent of parents and/or carers to share information directly with other relevant professionals.

Assessment at the end of the EYFS – the Early Years Foundation Stage Profile (EYFSP)

2.6. In the final term of the year in which the child reaches age five, and no later than 30 June in that term, the EYFS Profile must be completed for each child. The Profile provides parents and carers, practitioners and teachers with a well-rounded picture of a child's knowledge, understanding and abilities, their progress against expected levels, and their readiness for Year 1. The Profile must reflect: ongoing observation; all relevant records held by the setting; discussions with parents and carers, and any other adults whom the teacher, parent or carer judges can offer a useful contribution.

2.7. Each child's level of development must be assessed against the early learning goals (see Section 1). Practitioners must indicate whether children are meeting expected levels of development, or if they are exceeding expected levels, or not yet reaching expected levels ('emerging'). This is the EYFS Profile.

2.8. Year 1 teachers must be given a copy of the Profile report together with a short commentary on each child's skills and abilities in relation to the three key characteristics of effective learning (see paragraph 1.10). These should inform a dialogue between Reception and Year 1 teachers about each child's stage of development and learning needs and assist with the planning of activities in Year 1.

2.9. Schools[7] must share the results of the Profile with parents and/or carers, and explain to them when and how they can discuss the Profile with the teacher[8] who completed it. For children attending more than one setting, the Profile must be completed by the school where the child spends most time. If a child moves to a new school during the academic year, the original school must send their assessment of the child's level of development against the early learning goals to the relevant school within 15 days of receiving a request. If a child moves during the summer term, relevant providers must agree which of them will complete the Profile.

---

[7] Or the relevant provider.
[8] Or other practitioner.

2.10. The Profile must be completed for all children, including those with special educational needs or disabilities. Reasonable adjustments to the assessment process for children with special educational needs and disabilities must be made as appropriate. Providers should consider whether they may need to seek specialist assistance to help with this. Children will have differing levels of skills and abilities across the Profile and it is important that there is a full assessment of all areas of their development, to inform plans for future activities and to identify any additional support needs.

Information to be provided to the local authority

2.11. Early years providers must report EYFS Profile results to local authorities, upon request[9]. Local authorities are under a duty to return this data to the relevant Government department. Providers must permit the relevant local authority to enter their premises to observe the completion of the EYFS Profile, and permit the relevant local authority to examine and take copies of documents and other articles relating to the Profile and assessments[10]. Providers must take part in all reasonable moderation activities specified by their local authority and provide the local authority with such information relating to the EYFS Profile and assessment as they may reasonably request.

---

[9] Childcare (Provision of Information About Young Children) (England) Regulations 2009.
[10] The Early Years Foundation Stage (Learning and Development Requirements) Order 2007.

Section 3 – The safeguarding and welfare requirements

Introduction

3.1. Children learn best when they are healthy, safe and secure, when their individual needs are met, and when they have positive relationships with the adults caring for them. The safeguarding and welfare requirements, specified in this section, are designed to help providers create high quality settings which are welcoming, safe and stimulating, and where children are able to enjoy learning and grow in confidence.

3.2. Providers must take all necessary steps to keep children safe and well. The requirements in this section explain what early years providers must do to: safeguard children; ensure the suitability of adults who have contact with children; promote good health; manage behaviour; and maintain records, policies and procedures.

3.3. Schools are not required to have separate policies to cover EYFS requirements provided the requirements are already met through an existing policy. Where providers other than childminders are required to have policies and procedures as specified below, these policies and procedures should be recorded in writing. Childminders are not required to have written policies and procedures. However, they must be able to explain their policies and procedures to parents, carers, and others (for example Ofsted inspectors or the childminder agency with which they are registered) and ensure any assistants follow them.

Child protection

3.4. Providers must be alert to any issues for concern in the child's life at home or elsewhere. Providers must have and implement a policy, and procedures, to safeguard children. These should be in line with the guidance and procedures of the relevant Local Safeguarding Children Board (LSCB). The safeguarding policy and procedures must include an explanation of the action to be taken in the event of an allegation being made against a member of staff, and cover the use of mobile phones and cameras in the setting.

3.5. A practitioner must be designated to take lead responsibility for safeguarding children in every setting. Childminders must take the lead responsibility themselves. The lead practitioner is responsible for liaison with local statutory children's services agencies, and with the LSCB. They must provide support, advice and guidance to any other staff on an ongoing basis, and on any specific safeguarding issue as required. The lead practitioner must attend a child protection training course[11] that

---

[11] Taking account of any advice from the LSCB or local authority on appropriate training courses.

enables them to identify, understand and respond appropriately to signs of possible abuse and neglect (as described at paragraph 3.6).

3.6. Providers must train all staff to understand their safeguarding policy and procedures, and ensure that all staff have up to date knowledge of safeguarding issues. Training made available by the provider must enable staff to identify signs of possible abuse and neglect at the earliest opportunity, and to respond in a timely and appropriate way. These may include:

- significant changes in children's behaviour;

- deterioration in children's general well-being;

- unexplained bruising, marks or signs of possible abuse or neglect;

- children's comments which give cause for concern;

- any reasons to suspect neglect or abuse outside the setting, for example in the child's home; and/or

- inappropriate behaviour displayed by other members of staff, or any other person working with the children. For example: inappropriate sexual comments; excessive one-to-one attention beyond the requirements of their usual role and responsibilities; or inappropriate sharing of images.

3.7. Providers must have regard to the Government's statutory guidance 'Working Together to Safeguard Children 2013'. If providers have concerns about children's safety or welfare, they must notify agencies with statutory responsibilities without delay. This means the local children's social care services and, in emergencies, the police.

3.8. Registered providers must inform Ofsted or their childminder agency of any allegations of serious harm or abuse by any person living, working, or looking after children at the premises (whether the allegations relate to harm or abuse committed on the premises or elsewhere). Registered providers must also notify Ofsted or their childminder agency of the action taken in respect of the allegations. These notifications must be made as soon as is reasonably practicable, but at the latest within 14 days of the allegations being made. A registered provider who, without reasonable excuse, fails to comply with this requirement, commits an offence.

Suitable people

3.9. Providers must ensure that people looking after children are suitable to fulfil the requirements of their roles. Providers must have effective systems in place to ensure that practitioners, and any other person who is likely to have regular contact with children (including those living or working on the premises), are suitable[12].

3.10. Ofsted or the agency with which the childminder is registered is responsible for checking the suitability of childminders and of persons living or working on a childminder's premises, including obtaining enhanced criminal records checks and barred list checks. Providers other than childminders must obtain an enhanced criminal records disclosure in respect of every person aged 16 and over who[13]:

- works directly with children;

- lives on the premises on which the childcare is provided; and/or

- works on the premises on which the childcare is provided (unless they do not work on the part of the premises where the childcare takes place, or do not work there at times when children are present).

3.11. Providers must tell staff that they are expected to disclose any convictions, cautions, court orders, reprimands and warnings that may affect their suitability to work with children (whether received before or during their employment at the setting). Providers must not allow people whose suitability has not been checked, including through a criminal records check, to have unsupervised contact with children being cared for.

3.12. Providers other than childminders must record information about staff qualifications and the identity checks and vetting processes that have been completed (including the criminal records disclosure reference number, the date a disclosure was obtained and details of who obtained it). For childminders the relevant information will be kept by Ofsted or the agency with which the childminder is registered.

3.13. Providers must also meet their responsibilities under the Safeguarding Vulnerable Groups Act 2006, which includes a duty to make a referral to the Disclosure and Barring Service where a member of staff is dismissed (or would have been, had the person not left the setting first) because they have harmed a child or put a child at risk of harm[14].

---

[12] To allow Ofsted or the relevant childminder agency to make these checks, childminders are required to supply information to Ofsted or the relevant childminder agency, as set out in Schedule 1, Part 2 of the Childcare (Early Years Register) Regulations 2008, amended by the Childcare (Early Years Register) (Amendment) Regulations 2012. The requirements relating to people who live and work on childminder premises are in Schedule 1, Part 1.
[13] The requirement for a criminal records check will be deemed to have been met in respect of all people living or working in childcare settings, whose suitability was checked by Ofsted or their local authority before October 2005.
[14] Section 35 of the Safeguarding Vulnerable Groups Act 2006.

Disqualification (all registered providers and employees in registered settings)

3.14. A registered provider or a childcare worker may be disqualified from registration[15]. In the event of the disqualification of a registered provider, the provider must not continue as an early years provider – nor be directly concerned in the management of such provision. Where a person is disqualified, the provider must not employ that person in connection with early years provision. Where an employer becomes aware of relevant information that may lead to disqualification of an employee, the provider must take appropriate action to ensure the safety of children.

3.15. A registered provider or a childcare worker may also be disqualified because they live in the same household as another person who is disqualified, or because they live in the same household where a disqualified person is employed.

3.16. A provider must notify Ofsted or the agency with which the childminder is registered of any significant event which is likely to affect the suitability of any person who is in regular contact with children on the premises where childcare is provided. The disqualification of an employee could be an instance of a significant event. If a registered person or childcare worker is disqualified they may, in some circumstances, be able to obtain a 'waiver' from Ofsted.

3.17. The provider must give Ofsted or the childminder agency with which they are registered, the following information about themselves or about any person who lives in the same household as the registered provider or who is employed in the household:

- details of any order, determination, conviction, or other ground for disqualification from registration under regulations made under section 75 of the Childcare Act 2006;

- the date of the order, determination or conviction, or the date when the other ground for disqualification arose;

- the body or court which made the order, determination or conviction, and the sentence (if any) imposed; and

- a certified copy of the relevant order (in relation to an order or conviction).

3.18. The information must be provided to Ofsted or the childminder agency with which they are registered as soon as reasonably practicable, but at the latest within 14 days of the date the provider became aware of the information or ought reasonably to have become aware of it if they had made reasonable enquiries.

---

[15] In accordance with regulations made under Section 75 of the Childcare Act 2006.

Staff taking medication/other substances

3.19. Practitioners must not be under the influence of alcohol or any other substance which may affect their ability to care for children. If practitioners are taking medication which may affect their ability to care for children, those practitioners should seek medical advice. Providers must ensure that those practitioners only work directly with children if medical advice confirms that the medication is unlikely to impair that staff member's ability to look after children properly. Staff medication on the premises must be securely stored, and out of reach of children, at all times.

Staff qualifications, training, support and skills

3.20. The daily experience of children in early years settings and the overall quality of provision depends on all practitioners having appropriate qualifications, training, skills and knowledge and a clear understanding of their roles and responsibilities. Providers must ensure that all staff receive induction training to help them understand their roles and responsibilities. Induction training must include information about emergency evacuation procedures, safeguarding, child protection, the provider's equality policy, and health and safety issues. Providers must support staff to undertake appropriate training and professional development opportunities to ensure they offer quality learning and development experiences for children that continually improves.

3.21. Providers must put appropriate arrangements in place for the supervision of staff who have contact with children and families. Effective supervision provides support, coaching and training for the practitioner and promotes the interests of children. Supervision should foster a culture of mutual support, teamwork and continuous improvement, which encourages the confidential discussion of sensitive issues.

3.22. Supervision should provide opportunities for staff to:

- discuss any issues – particularly concerning children's development or well-being;

- identify solutions to address issues as they arise; and

- receive coaching to improve their personal effectiveness.

3.23. In group settings, the manager must hold at least a full and relevant[16] level 3[17] qualification and at least half of all other staff must hold at least a full and relevant level 2 qualification. The manager should have at least two years' experience of working in an early years setting, or have at least two years' other suitable experience. The provider must ensure there is a named deputy who, in their judgement, is capable and qualified to take charge in the manager's absence.

---

[16] As defined by the National College for Teaching and Leadership.
[17] To count in the ratios at level 3, staff holding an Early Years Educator qualification must also have achieved GCSEs in English and maths at grade C or above.

3.24. Childminders must have completed training which helps them to understand and implement the EYFS before they can register with Ofsted or a childminder agency. Childminders are accountable for the quality of the work of any assistants, and must be satisfied that assistants are competent in the areas of work they undertake.

3.25. At least one person who has a current paediatric first aid certificate must be on the premises and available at all times when children are present, and must accompany children on outings. Childminders, and any assistant who might be in sole charge of the children for any period of time, must hold a current paediatric first aid certificate. Paediatric first aid training[18] must be relevant for workers caring for young children and where relevant, babies. Providers should take into account the number of children, staff and layout of premises to ensure that a paediatric first aider is able to respond to emergencies quickly.

3.26. Providers must ensure that staff have sufficient understanding and use of English to ensure the well-being of children in their care. For example, settings must be in a position to keep records in English, to liaise with other agencies in English, to summon emergency help, and to understand instructions such as those for the safety of medicines or food hygiene.

Key person

3.27. Each child must be assigned a key person. Their role is to help ensure that every child's care is tailored to meet their individual needs (in accordance with paragraph 1.10), to help the child become familiar with the setting, offer a settled relationship for the child and build a relationship with their parents.

Staff:child ratios

3.28. Staffing arrangements must meet the needs of all children and ensure their safety. Providers must ensure that children are adequately supervised and decide how to deploy staff to ensure children's needs are met. Providers must inform parents and/or carers about staff deployment, and, when relevant and practical, aim to involve them in these decisions. Children must usually be within sight and hearing of staff and always within sight or hearing.

3.29. Only those aged 17 or over may be included in ratios (and staff under 17 should be supervised at all times). Students on long term placements and volunteers (aged 17 or over) and staff working as apprentices in early education (aged 16 or over) may be included in the ratios if the provider is satisfied that they are competent and responsible.

---

[18] Providers can choose which organisation they wish to provide the training (preferably one with a nationally approved and accredited first aid qualification or one that is a member of a trade body with an approval and monitoring scheme) but the training must cover the course content as for St John Ambulance or Red Cross **paediatric** first aid training and be renewed every three years.

3.30. The ratio and qualification requirements below apply to the total number of staff available to work directly with children[19]. For group settings providing overnight care, the relevant ratios continue to apply and at least one member of staff must be awake at all times. Exceptionally, and where the quality of care and safety and security of children is maintained, changes to the ratios may be made.

Early years providers (other than childminders)

3.31. For children aged under two:

- there must be at least one member of staff for every three children;

- at least one member of staff must hold a full and relevant level 3 qualification, and must be suitably experienced in working with children under two;

- at least half of all other staff must hold a full and relevant level 2 qualification;

- at least half of all staff must have received training that specifically addresses the care of babies; and

- where there is an under two-year-olds' room, the member of staff in charge of that room must, in the judgement of the provider, have suitable experience of working with under twos.

3.32. For children aged two:

- there must be at least one member of staff for every four children;

- at least one member of staff must hold a full and relevant level 3 qualification; and

- at least half of all other staff must hold a full and relevant level 2 qualification.

3.33. For children aged three and over in registered early years provision where a person with Qualified Teacher Status, Early Years Professional Status, Early Years Teacher Status or another suitable level 6 qualification is working directly with the children[20]:

- there must be at least one member of staff for every 13 children; and

- at least one other member of staff must hold a full and relevant level 3 qualification.

3.34. For children aged three and over at any time in registered early years provision when a person with Qualified Teacher Status, Early Years Professional Status,

---

[19] Ofsted may determine that providers must observe a higher staff:child ratio than outlined here to ensure the safety and welfare of children.
[20] We expect the teacher (or equivalent) to be working with children for the vast majority of the time. Where they need to be absent for short periods of time, the provider will need to ensure that quality and safety is maintained.

Early Years Teacher Status or another suitable level 6 qualification is not working directly with the children:

- there must be at least one member of staff for every eight children;
- at least one member of staff must hold a full and relevant level 3 qualification;
- at least half of all other staff must hold a full and relevant level 2 qualification.

3.35. For children aged three and over in independent schools, where a person with Qualified Teacher Status, Early Years Professional Status, Early Years Teacher Status or another suitable level 6 qualification, an instructor[21], or another suitably qualified overseas trained teacher, is working directly with the children:

- for classes where the majority of children will reach the age of five or older within the school year, there must be at least one member of staff for every 30 children;
- for all other classes there must be at least one member of staff for every 13 children; and
- at least one other member of staff must hold a full and relevant level 3 qualification.

3.36. For children aged three and over in independent schools, where there is no person with Qualified Teacher Status, Early Years Professional Status, Early Years Teacher Status or another suitable level 6 qualification, no instructor, and no suitably qualified overseas trained teacher, working directly with the children:

- there must be at least one member of staff for every eight children;
- at least one member of staff must hold a full and relevant level 3 qualification; and
- at least half of all other staff must hold a full and relevant level 2 qualification.

3.37. For children aged three and over in maintained nursery schools and nursery classes in maintained schools:

- there must be at least one member of staff for every 13 children[22];
- at least one member of staff must be a school teacher as defined by section 122 of the Education Act 2002[23]; and

---

[21] An instructor is a person at the school who provides education which consists of instruction in any art or skill, or in any subject or group of subjects, in circumstances where:
(a) special qualifications or experience or both are required for such instruction, and
(b) the person or body of persons responsible for the management of the school is satisfied as to the qualifications or experience (or both) of the person providing education.
[22] Where children in nursery classes attend school for longer than the school day or in the school holidays, in provision run directly by the governing body or the proprietor, with no teacher present, a ratio of one member of staff to every eight children can be applied if at least one member of staff holds a full and relevant level 3 qualification, and at least half of all other staff hold a full and relevant level 2 qualification.
[23] See also the Education (School Teachers' Prescribed Qualifications, etc) Order 2003 and the Education (School Teachers' Qualifications) (England) Regulations 2003.

- at least one other member of staff must hold a full and relevant level 3 qualification.

3.38. Reception classes in maintained schools are subject to infant class size legislation. The School Admissions (Infant Class Size) Regulations 2012 limit the size of infant classes to 30 pupils per school teacher[24] while an ordinary teaching session is conducted. 'School teachers' do not include teaching assistants, higher level teaching assistants or other support staff. Consequently, in an ordinary teaching session, a school must employ sufficient school teachers to enable it to teach its infant classes in groups of no more than 30 per school teacher[25].

3.39. Some schools may choose to mix their reception classes with groups of younger children, in which case they must determine ratios within mixed groups, guided by all relevant ratio requirements and by the needs of individual children within the group. In exercising this discretion, the school must comply with the statutory requirements relating to the education of children of compulsory school age and infant class sizes. Schools' partner providers must meet the relevant ratio requirements for their provision.

Before/after school care and holiday provision

3.40. Where the provision is solely before/after school care or holiday provision for children who normally attend Reception class (or older) during the school day, there must be sufficient staff as for a class of 30 children. It is for providers to determine how many staff are needed to ensure the safety and welfare of children, bearing in mind the type(s) of activity and the age and needs of the children. It is also for providers to determine what qualifications, if any, the manager and/or staff should have. Providers do not need to meet the learning and development requirements in Section 1. However, practitioners should discuss with parents and/or carers (and other practitioners/providers as appropriate, including school staff/teachers) the support they intend to offer.

Childminders

3.41. At any one time, childminders may care for a maximum of six children under the age of eight[26]. Of these six children, a maximum of three may be young children, and there should only be one child under the age of one. A child is a young child up until 1st September following his or her fifth birthday. Any care provided for older

---

[24] As defined by section 122 of the Education Act 2002.

[25] In respect of school teachers' non-contact time, the Specified Work Regulations 2012 allow a non-teacher to carry out the work of the teacher ("specified work") where the non-teacher is assisting or supporting the work of the teacher, is subject to the teacher's direction and supervision as arranged with the head teacher, and the head teacher is satisfied that that person has the skills, expertise and experience required to carry out the specified work.

[26] Including the childminder's own children or any other children for whom they are responsible such as those being fostered.

children must not adversely affect the care of children receiving early years provision.

3.42. If a childminder can demonstrate to parents and/or carers and Ofsted inspectors or their childminder agency that the individual needs of all the children are being met, exceptions to the usual ratios can be made when childminders are caring for sibling babies, or when caring for their own baby. If children aged four and five only attend the childminding setting before and/or after a normal school day, and/or during school holidays, they may be cared for at the same time as three other young children. But in all circumstances, the total number of children under the age of eight being cared for must not exceed six.

3.43. If a childminder employs an assistant or works with another childminder, each childminder (or assistant) may care for the number of children permitted by the ratios specified above[27]. Children may be left in the sole care of childminders' assistants for two hours at most in a single day[28]. Childminders must obtain parents and/or carers' permission to leave children with an assistant, including for very short periods of time. For childminders providing overnight care, the ratios continue to apply and the childminder must always be able to hear the children (this may be via a monitor).

Health

Medicines

3.44. The provider must promote the good health of children attending the setting. They must have a procedure, discussed with parents and/or carers, for responding to children who are ill or infectious, take necessary steps to prevent the spread of infection, and take appropriate action if children are ill.

3.45. Providers must have and implement a policy, and procedures, for administering medicines. It must include systems for obtaining information about a child's needs for medicines, and for keeping this information up-to-date. Training must be provided for staff where the administration of medicine requires medical or technical knowledge. Medicines must not usually be administered unless they have been prescribed for a child by a doctor, dentist, nurse or pharmacist (medicines containing aspirin should only be given if prescribed by a doctor).

3.46. Medicine (both prescription and non-prescription) must only be administered to a child where written permission for that particular medicine has been obtained from the child's parent and/or carer. Providers must keep a written record each time a medicine is administered to a child, and inform the child's parents and/or carers on the same day, or as soon as reasonably practicable.

---

[27] Subject to any restrictions imposed by Ofsted or the relevant childminder agency on registration.
[28] The Childcare (Exemptions from Registration) Order 2008 specifies that where provision is made for a particular child for two hours or less a day, the carer is exempt from registration as a childminder.

Food and drink

3.47. Where children are provided with meals, snacks and drinks, they must be healthy, balanced and nutritious. Before a child is admitted to the setting the provider must also obtain information about any special dietary requirements, preferences and food allergies that the child has, and any special health requirements. Fresh drinking water must be available and accessible at all times. Providers must record and act on information from parents and carers about a child's dietary needs.

3.48. There must be an area which is adequately equipped to provide healthy meals, snacks and drinks for children as necessary. There must be suitable facilities for the hygienic preparation of food for children, if necessary including suitable sterilisation equipment for babies' food. Providers must be confident that those responsible for preparing and handling food are competent to do so. In group provision, all staff involved in preparing and handling food must receive training in food hygiene.

3.49. Registered providers must notify Ofsted or the childminder agency with which they are registered of any food poisoning affecting two or more children cared for on the premises. Notification must be made as soon as is reasonably practicable, but in any event within 14 days of the incident. A registered provider, who, without reasonable excuse, fails to comply with this requirement, commits an offence.

Accident or injury

3.50. Providers must ensure there is a first aid box accessible at all times with appropriate content for use with children. Providers must keep a written record of accidents or injuries and first aid treatment. Providers must inform parents and/or carers of any accident or injury sustained by the child on the same day, or as soon as reasonably practicable, of any first aid treatment given.

3.51. Registered providers must notify Ofsted or the childminder agency with which they are registered of any serious accident, illness or injury to, or death of, any child while in their care, and of the action taken. Notification must be made as soon as is reasonably practicable, but in any event within 14 days of the incident occurring. A registered provider, who, without reasonable excuse, fails to comply with this requirement, commits an offence. Providers must notify local child protection agencies of any serious accident or injury to, or the death of, any child while in their care, and must act on any advice from those agencies.

Managing behaviour

3.52. Providers are responsible for managing children's behaviour in an appropriate way. Providers must not give corporal punishment to a child. Providers must take all reasonable steps to ensure that corporal punishment is not given by any person who cares for or is in regular contact with a child, or by any person living or working in the premises where care is provided. Any early years provider who fails to meet these requirements commits an offence. A person will not be taken to have used corporal punishment (and therefore will not have committed an offence), where physical intervention[29] was taken for the purposes of averting immediate danger of personal injury to any person (including the child) or to manage a child's behaviour if absolutely necessary. Providers, including childminders, must keep a record of any occasion where physical intervention is used, and parents and/or carers must be informed on the same day, or as soon as reasonably practicable.

3.53. Providers must not threaten corporal punishment, and must not use or threaten any punishment which could adversely affect a child's well-being.

Safety and suitability of premises, environment and equipment

Safety

3.54. Providers must ensure that their premises, including overall floor space and outdoor spaces, are fit for purpose and suitable for the age of children cared for and the activities provided on the premises. Providers must comply with requirements of health and safety legislation (including fire safety and hygiene requirements).

3.55. Providers must take reasonable steps to ensure the safety of children, staff and others on the premises in the case of fire or any other emergency, and must have an emergency evacuation procedure. Providers must have appropriate fire detection and control equipment (for example, fire alarms, smoke detectors, fire blankets and/or fire extinguishers) which is in working order. Fire exits must be clearly identifiable, and fire doors must be free of obstruction and easily opened from the inside.

Smoking

3.56. Providers must not allow smoking in or on the premises when children are present or about to be present.

Premises

3.57. The premises and equipment must be organised in a way that meets the needs of children. In registered provision, providers must meet the following indoor space requirements[30]:

- Children under two years: 3.5 m^2 per child.

---

[29] Physical intervention is where practitioners use reasonable force to prevent children from injuring themselves or others or damaging property.
[30] These calculations should be based on the net or useable areas of the rooms used by the children, not including storage areas, thoroughfares, dedicated staff areas, cloakrooms, utility rooms, kitchens and toilets.

- Two year olds: 2.5 m^2 per child.

- Children aged three to five years: 2.3 m^2 per child.

3.58. Providers must provide access to an outdoor play area or, if that is not possible, ensure that outdoor activities are planned and taken on a daily basis (unless circumstances make this inappropriate, for example unsafe weather conditions). Providers must follow their legal responsibilities under the Equality Act 2010 (for example, the provisions on reasonable adjustments).

3.59. Sleeping children must be frequently checked. Except in childminding settings, there should be a separate baby room for children under the age of two. However, providers must ensure that children in a baby room have contact with older children and are moved into the older age group when appropriate.

3.60. Providers must ensure there is an adequate number of toilets and hand basins available. Except in childminding settings, there should usually be separate toilet facilities for adults. Providers must ensure there are suitable hygienic changing facilities for changing any children who are in nappies and providers should ensure that an adequate supply of clean bedding, towels, spare clothes and any other necessary items is always available.

3.61. Providers must also ensure that there is an area where staff may talk to parents and/or carers confidentially, as well as an area in group settings for staff to take breaks away from areas being used by children.

3.62. Providers must only release children into the care of individuals who have been notified to the provider by the parent, and must ensure that children do not leave the premises unsupervised. Providers must take all reasonable steps to prevent unauthorised persons entering the premises, and have an agreed procedure for checking the identity of visitors. Providers must consider what additional measures are necessary when children stay overnight.

3.63. Providers must carry public liability insurance.

Risk assessment

3.64. Providers must ensure that they take all reasonable steps to ensure staff and children in their care are not exposed to risks and must be able to demonstrate how they are managing risks[31]. Providers must determine where it is helpful to make some written risk assessments in relation to specific issues, to inform staff practice, and to demonstrate how they are managing risks if asked by parents and/or carers or inspectors. Risk assessments should identify aspects of the environment that need to be checked on a regular basis, when and by whom those aspects will be checked, and how the risk will be removed or minimised.

---

[31] Guidance on risk assessments, including where written ones may be required where five or more staff are employed, can be obtained from the Health and Safety Executive.

Outings

3.65. Children must be kept safe while on outings. Providers must assess the risks or hazards which may arise for the children, and must identify the steps to be taken to remove, minimise and manage those risks and hazards. The assessment must include consideration of adult to child ratios. The risk assessment does not necessarily need to be in writing; this is for providers to judge.

3.66. Vehicles in which children are being transported, and the driver of those vehicles, must be adequately insured.

Special educational needs

3.67. Providers must have arrangements in place to support children with SEN or disabilities. Maintained nursery schools and other providers who are funded by the local authority to deliver early education places must have regard to the Special Educational Needs (SEN) Code of Practice[32]. Maintained nursery schools must identify a member of staff to act as Special Educational Needs Co-ordinator[33] and other providers (in group provision) are expected to identify a SENCO.

Information and records

3.68. Providers must maintain records and obtain and share information (with parents and carers, other professionals working with the child, the police, social services and Ofsted or the childminder agency with which they are registered, as appropriate) to ensure the safe and efficient management of the setting, and to help ensure the needs of all children are met. Providers must enable a regular two-way flow of information with parents and/or carers, and between providers, if a child is attending more than one setting. If requested, providers should incorporate parents' and/or carers' comments into children's records.

3.69. Records must be easily accessible and available (with prior agreement from Ofsted or the childminder agency with which they are registered, these may be kept securely off the premises). Confidential information and records about staff and children must be held securely and only accessible and available to those who have a right or professional need to see them. Providers must be aware of their responsibilities under the Data Protection Act (DPA) 1998 and where relevant the Freedom of Information Act 2000.

3.70. Providers must ensure that all staff understand the need to protect the privacy of the children in their care as well the legal requirements that exist to ensure that information relating to the child is handled in a way that ensures confidentiality.

---

[32] See section 77(1)(g) and (4) of the Children and Families Act 2014.
[33] See section 67(2) and 67(3) of the Children and Families Act 2014.

Parents and/or carers must be given access to all records about their child, provided that no relevant exemptions apply to their disclosure under the DPA[34].

3.71. Records relating to individual children must be retained for a reasonable period of time after they have left the provision.

Information about the child

3.72. Providers must record the following information for each child in their care: full name; date of birth; name and address of every parent and/or carer who is known to the provider (and information about any other person who has parental responsibility for the child); which parent(s) and/or carer(s) the child normally lives with; and emergency contact details for parents and/or carers.

Information for parents and carers

3.73. Providers must make the following information available to parents and/or carers:

- how the EYFS is being delivered in the setting, and how parents and/or carers can access more information;

- the range and type of activities and experiences provided for children, the daily routines of the setting, and how parents and carers can share learning at home;

- how the setting supports children with special educational needs and disabilities;

- food and drinks provided for children;

- details of the provider's policies and procedures (all providers except childminders must make copies available on request) including the procedure to be followed in the event of a parent and/or carer failing to collect a child at the appointed time, or in the event of a child going missing at, or away from, the setting; and

- staffing in the setting; the name of their child's key person and their role; and a telephone number for parents and/or carers to contact in an emergency.

Complaints

3.74. Providers must put in place a written procedure for dealing with concerns and complaints from parents and/or carers, and must keep a written record of any complaints, and their outcome. Childminders are not required to have a written procedure for handling complaints, but they must keep a record of any complaints

---

[34] The Data Protection Act 1998 (DPA) gives parents and carers the right to access information about their child that a provider holds. However, the DPA also sets out specific exemptions under which certain personal information may, under specific circumstances, be withheld from release. For example, a relevant professional will need to give careful consideration as to whether the disclosure of certain information about a child could cause harm either to the child or any other individual. It is therefore essential that all providers/staff in early years settings have an understanding of how data protection laws operate. Further guidance can be found on the website of the Information Commissioner's Office at: http://www.ico.gov.uk/for_organisations/data_protection.aspx .

they receive and their outcome. All providers must investigate written complaints relating to their fulfillment of the EYFS requirements and notify complainants of the outcome of the investigation within 28 days of having received the complaint. The record of complaints must be made available to Ofsted or the relevant childminder agency on request.

3.75. Providers must make available to parents and/or carers details about how to contact Ofsted or the childminder agency with which the provider is registered as appropriate, if they believe the provider is not meeting the EYFS requirements. If providers become aware that they are to be inspected by Ofsted or have a quality assurance visit by the childminder agency, they must notify parents and/or carers. After an inspection by Ofsted or a quality assurance visit by their childminder agency, providers must supply a copy of the report to parents and/or carers of children attending on a regular basis.

Information about the provider

3.76. Providers must hold the following documentation:

- name, home address and telephone number of the provider and any other person living or employed on the premises (this requirement does not apply to childminders);

- name, home address and telephone number of anyone else who will regularly be in unsupervised contact with the children attending the early years provision;

- a daily record of the names of the children being cared for on the premises, their hours of attendance and the names of each child's key person; and

- their certificate of registration (which must be displayed at the setting and shown to parents and/or carers on request).

Changes that must be notified to Ofsted or the relevant childminder agency

3.77. All registered early years providers must notify Ofsted or the childminder agency with which they are registered of:

- any change in the address of the premises; to the premises which may affect the space available to children and the quality of childcare available to them; in the name or address of the provider, or the provider's other contact information; to the person who is managing the early years provision; or in the persons aged 16 years or older living or working on childminding premises;[35]

---

[35] A person is not considered to be working on the premises if none of their work is done in the part of the premises in which children are cared for, or if they do not work on the premises at times when children are there.

- any proposal to change the hours during which childcare is provided; or to provide overnight care;

- any significant event which is likely to affect the suitability of the early years provider or any person who cares for, or is in regular contact with, children on the premises to look after children;

- where the early years provision is provided by a company, any change in the name or registered number of the company;

- where the early years provision is provided by a charity, any change in the name or registration number of the charity;

- where the childcare is provided by a partnership, body corporate or unincorporated association, any change to the 'nominated individual'; and

- where the childcare is provided by a partnership, body corporate or unincorporated association whose sole or main purpose is the provision of childcare, any change to the individuals who are partners in, or a director, secretary or other officer or members of its governing body.

3.78. Where providers are required to notify Ofsted or their childminder agency about a change of person except for managers, as specified in paragraph 3.76 above, providers must give Ofsted or their childminder agency the new person's name, any former names or aliases, date of birth, and home address. If there is a change of manager, providers must notify Ofsted or their childminder agency that a new manager has been appointed. Where it is reasonably practicable to do so, notification must be made in advance. In other cases, notification must be made as soon as is reasonably practicable, but always within 14 days. A registered provider who, without reasonable excuse, fails to comply with these requirements commits an offence.

Early years outcomes

A non-statutory guide for practitioners and inspectors to help inform understanding of child development through the early years

September 2013

Introduction

The Early Years Foundation Stage (EYFS) requires early years practitioners to review children's progress and share a summary with parents at two points:

- between the ages of 24 and 36 months via the progress check; and
- at the end of reception via the EYFS profile.

This document is a non-statutory guide to support practitioners. It can be used by childminders, nurseries and others, such as Ofsted, throughout the early years as a guide to making best-fit judgements about whether a child is showing typical development for their age, may be at risk of delay or is ahead for their age.

1. Communication and language

The tables below set out what you should be observing a child doing at each stage, if they are developing typically for their age.

Listening and attention

Age	Typical behaviour
Birth to 11 months	• Turns towards a familiar sound then locates range of sounds with accuracy. • Listens to, distinguishes and responds to intonations and sounds of voices. • Reacts in interaction with others by smiling, looking and moving. • Quietens or alerts to the sound of speech. • Looks intently at a person talking, but stops responding if speaker turns away. • Listens to familiar sounds, words, or finger plays. • Fleeting Attention – not under child's control, new stimuli takes whole attention.
8 to 20 months	• Moves whole bodies to sounds they enjoy, such as music or a regular beat. • Has a strong exploratory impulse. • Concentrates intently on an object or activity of own choosing for short periods. • Pays attention to dominant stimulus – easily distracted by noises or other people talking.
16 to 26 months	• Listens to and enjoys rhythmic patterns in rhymes and stories. • Enjoys rhymes and demonstrates listening by trying to join in with actions or vocalisations. • Rigid attention – may appear not to hear.
22 to 36 months	• Listens with interest to the noises adults make when they read stories. • Recognises and responds to many familiar sounds, e.g.

Age	Typical behaviour
	turning to a knock on the door, looking at or going to the door. • Shows interest in play with sounds, songs and rhymes. • Single channelled attention. Can shift to a different task if attention fully obtained – using child's name helps focus.
30 to 50 months	• Listens to others one to one or in small groups, when conversation interests them. • Listens to stories with increasing attention and recall. • Joins in with repeated refrains and anticipates key events and phrases in rhymes and stories. • Focusing attention – still listen or do, but can shift own attention. • Is able to follow directions (if not intently focused on own choice of activity).
40 to 60+ months	• Maintains attention, concentrates and sits quietly during appropriate activity. • Two-channelled attention – can listen and do for short span.

Early learning goal – listening and attention

Children listen attentively in a range of situations. They listen to stories, accurately anticipating key events and respond to what they hear with relevant comments, questions or actions. They give their attention to what others say and respond appropriately, while engaged in another activity.

Understanding

Age	Typical behaviour
Birth to 11 months	• Stops and looks when hears own name. • Starts to understand contextual clues, e.g. familiar gestures, words and sounds.

8 to 20 months	• Developing the ability to follow others' body language, including pointing and gesture. • Responds to the different things said when in a familiar context with a special person (e.g. 'Where's Mummy?', Where's your nose?'). • Understanding of single words in context is developing, e.g. 'cup', 'milk', 'daddy'.
16 to 26 months	• Selects familiar objects by name and will go and find objects when asked, or identify objects from a group. • Understands simple sentences (e.g. 'Throw the ball'.)
22 to 36 months	• Identifies action words by pointing to the right picture, e.g. "Who's jumping?" • Understands more complex sentences, e.g. 'Put your toys away and then we'll read a book.' • Understands 'who', 'what', 'where' in simple questions (e.g. who's that? What's that? Where is?). • Developing understanding of simple concepts (e.g. big/little).
30 to 50 months	• Understands use of objects (e.g. "What do we use to cut things?') • Shows understanding of prepositions such as 'under', 'on top', 'behind' by carrying out an action or selecting correct picture. • Responds to simple instructions, e.g. to get or put away an object. • Beginning to understand 'why' and 'how' questions.
40 to 60+ months	• Responds to instructions involving a two-part sequence. • Understands humour, e.g. nonsense rhymes, jokes. • Able to follow a story without pictures or props. • Listens and responds to ideas expressed by others in conversation or discussion.

Early learning goal – understanding

Children follow instructions involving several ideas or actions. They answer 'how' and 'why' questions about their experiences and in response to stories or events.

Speaking

Age	Typical behaviour
Birth to 11 months	• Communicates needs and feelings in a variety of ways including crying, gurgling, babbling and squealing. • Makes own sounds in response when talked to by familiar adults. • Lifts arms in anticipation of being picked up. • Practises and gradually develops speech sounds (babbling) to communicate with adults; says sounds like 'baba, nono, gogo'.
8 to 20 months	• Uses sounds in play, e.g. 'brrrm' for toy car. • Uses single words. • Frequently imitates words and sounds. • Enjoys babbling and increasingly experiments with using sounds and words to communicate for a range of purposes (e.g. teddy, more, no, bye-bye.) • Uses pointing with eye gaze to make requests, and to share an interest. • Creates personal words as they begin to develop language.
16 to 26 months	• Copies familiar expressions, e.g. 'Oh dear', 'All gone'. • Beginning to put two words together (e.g. 'want ball', 'more juice'). • Uses different types of everyday words (nouns, verbs and adjectives, e.g. banana, go, sleep, hot). • Beginning to ask simple questions. • Beginning to talk about people and things that are not present.

22 to 36 months	• Uses language as a powerful means of widening contacts, sharing feelings, experiences and thoughts. • Holds a conversation, jumping from topic to topic. • Learns new words very rapidly and is able to use them in communicating. • Uses gestures, sometimes with limited talk, e.g. reaches towards toy, saying 'I have it'. • Uses a variety of questions (e.g. what, where, who). • Uses simple sentences (e.g.' Mummy gonna work.') • Beginning to use word endings (e.g. going, cats).
30 to 50 months	• Beginning to use more complex sentences to link thoughts (e.g. using and, because). • Can retell a simple past event in correct order (e.g. went down slide, hurt finger). • Uses talk to connect ideas, explain what is happening and anticipate what might happen next, recall and relive past experiences. • Questions why things happen and gives explanations. Asks e.g. who, what, when, how. • Uses a range of tenses (e.g. play, playing, will play, played). • Uses intonation, rhythm and phrasing to make the meaning clear to others. • Uses vocabulary focused on objects and people that are of particular importance to them. • Builds up vocabulary that reflects the breadth of their experiences. • Uses talk in pretending that objects stand for something else in play, e.g. 'This box is my castle.'
40 to 60+ months	• Extends vocabulary, especially by grouping and naming, exploring the meaning and sounds of new words. • Uses language to imagine and recreate roles and experiences in play situations. • Links statements and sticks to a main theme or intention. • Uses talk to organise, sequence and clarify thinking, ideas, feelings and events. • Introduces a storyline or narrative into their play.

Early learning goal – speaking

Children express themselves effectively, showing awareness of listeners' needs. They use past, present and future forms accurately when talking about events that have happened or are to happen in the future. They develop their own narratives and explanations by connecting ideas or events.

2. Physical development

The tables below set out what you should be observing a child doing at each stage, if they are developing typically for their age.

Moving and handling

Age	Typical behaviour
Birth to 11 months	<ul><li>Turns head in response to sounds and sights.</li><li>Gradually develops ability to hold up own head.</li><li>Makes movements with arms and legs which gradually become more controlled.</li><li>Rolls over from front to back, from back to front.</li><li>When lying on tummy becomes able to lift first head and then chest, supporting self with forearms and then straight arms.</li><li>Watches and explores hands and feet, e.g. when lying on back lifts legs into vertical position and grasps feet.</li><li>Reaches out for, touches and begins to hold objects.</li><li>Explores objects with mouth, often picking up an object and holding it to the mouth.</li></ul>
8 to 20 months	<ul><li>Sits unsupported on the floor.</li><li>When sitting, can lean forward to pick up small toys.</li><li>Pulls to standing, holding on to furniture or person for support.</li><li>Crawls, bottom shuffles or rolls continuously to move around.</li><li>Walks around furniture lifting one foot and stepping sideways (cruising), and walks with one or both hands held by adult.</li><li>Takes first few steps independently.</li><li>Passes toys from one hand to the other.</li><li>Holds an object in each hand and brings them together in the middle, e.g. holds two blocks and bangs them together.</li><li>Picks up small objects between thumb and fingers.</li><li>Enjoys the sensory experience of making marks in damp sand, paste or paint.</li><li>Holds pen or crayon using a whole hand (palmar) grasp and makes random marks with different strokes.</li></ul>

16 to 26 months	<ul><li>Walks upstairs holding hand of adult.</li><li>Comes downstairs backwards on knees (crawling).</li><li>Beginning to balance blocks to build a small tower.</li><li>Makes connections between their movement and the marks they make.</li></ul>
22 to 36 months	<ul><li>Runs safely on whole foot.</li><li>Squats with steadiness to rest or play with object on the ground, and rises to feet without using hands.</li><li>Climbs confidently and is beginning to pull themselves up on nursery play climbing equipment.</li><li>Can kick a large ball.</li><li>Turns pages in a book, sometimes several at once.</li><li>Shows control in holding and using jugs to pour, hammers, books and mark-making tools.</li><li>Beginning to use three fingers (tripod grip) to hold writing tools.</li><li>Imitates drawing simple shapes such as circles and lines.</li><li>Walks upstairs or downstairs holding onto a rail two feet to a step.</li><li>May be beginning to show preference for dominant hand.</li></ul>
30 to 50 months	<ul><li>Moves freely and with pleasure and confidence in a range of ways, such as slithering, shuffling, rolling, crawling, walking, running, jumping, skipping, sliding and hopping.</li><li>Mounts stairs, steps or climbing equipment using alternate feet.</li><li>Walks downstairs, two feet to each step while carrying a small object.</li><li>Runs skilfully and negotiates space successfully, adjusting speed or direction to avoid obstacles.</li><li>Can stand momentarily on one foot when shown.</li><li>Can catch a large ball.</li><li>Draws lines and circles using gross motor movements.</li><li>Uses one-handed tools and equipment, e.g. makes snips in paper with child scissors.</li><li>Holds pencil between thumb and two fingers, no longer using whole-hand grasp.</li><li>Holds pencil near point between first two fingers and thumb</li></ul>

	and uses it with good control. • Can copy some letters, e.g. letters from their name.
40 to 60+ months	• Experiments with different ways of moving. • Jumps off an object and lands appropriately. • Negotiates space successfully when playing racing and chasing games with other children, adjusting speed or changing direction to avoid obstacles. • Travels with confidence and skill around, under, over and through balancing and climbing equipment. • Shows increasing control over an object in pushing, patting, throwing, catching or kicking it. • Uses simple tools to effect changes to materials. • Handles tools, objects, construction and malleable materials safely and with increasing control. • Shows a preference for a dominant hand. • Begins to use anticlockwise movement and retrace vertical lines. • Begins to form recognisable letters. • Uses a pencil and holds it effectively to form recognisable letters, most of which are correctly formed.

Early learning goal – moving and handling

Children show good control and co-ordination in large and small movements. They move confidently in a range of ways, safely negotiating space. They handle equipment and tools effectively, including pencils for writing.

Health and self-care

Age	Typical behaviour
Birth to 11 months	<ul><li>Responds to and thrives on warm, sensitive physical contact and care.</li><li>Expresses discomfort, hunger or thirst.</li><li>Anticipates food routines with interest.</li></ul>
8 to 20 months	<ul><li>Opens mouth for spoon.</li><li>Holds own bottle or cup.</li><li>Grasps finger foods and brings them to mouth.</li><li>Attempts to use spoon: can guide towards mouth but food often falls off.</li><li>Can actively cooperate with nappy changing (lies still, helps hold legs up).</li><li>Starts to communicate urination, bowel movement.</li></ul>
16 to 26 months	<ul><li>Develops own likes and dislikes in food and drink.</li><li>Willing to try new food textures and tastes.</li><li>Holds cup with both hands and drinks without much spilling.</li><li>Clearly communicates wet or soiled nappy or pants.</li><li>Shows some awareness of bladder and bowel urges.</li><li>Shows awareness of what a potty or toilet is used for.</li><li>Shows a desire to help with dressing/undressing and hygiene routines.</li></ul>
22 to 36 months	<ul><li>Feeds self competently with spoon.</li><li>Drinks well without spilling.</li><li>Clearly communicates their need for potty or toilet.</li><li>Beginning to recognise danger and seeks support of significant adults for help.</li><li>Helps with clothing, e.g. puts on hat, unzips zipper on jacket, takes off unbuttoned shirt.</li><li>Beginning to be independent in self-care, but still often needs adult support.</li></ul>

30 to 50 months	• Can tell adults when hungry or tired or when they want to rest or play. • Observes the effects of activity on their bodies. • Understands that equipment and tools have to be used safely. • Gains more bowel and bladder control and can attend to toileting needs most of the time themselves. • Can usually manage washing and drying hands. • Dresses with help, e.g. puts arms into open-fronted coat or shirt when held up, pulls up own trousers, and pulls up zipper once it is fastened at the bottom.
40 to 60+ months	• Eats a healthy range of foodstuffs and understands need for variety in food. • Usually dry and clean during the day. • Shows some understanding that good practices with regard to exercise, eating, sleeping and hygiene can contribute to good health. • Shows understanding of the need for safety when tackling new challenges, and considers and manages some risks. • Shows understanding of how to transport and store equipment safely. • Practices some appropriate safety measures without direct supervision.

Early learning goal – health and self-care

Children know the importance for good health of physical exercise, and a healthy diet, and talk about ways to keep healthy and safe. They manage their own basic hygiene and personal needs successfully, including dressing and going to the toilet independently.

3. Personal, social and emotional development

The tables below set out what you should be observing a child doing at each stage, if they are developing typically for their age.

Self-confidence and self-awareness

Age	Typical behaviour
Birth to 11 months	• Laughs and gurgles, e.g. shows pleasure at being tickled and other physical interactions. • Uses voice, gesture, eye contact and facial expression to make contact with people and keep their attention.
8 to 20 months	• Enjoys finding own nose, eyes or tummy as part of naming games. • Learns that own voice and actions have effects on others. • Uses pointing with eye gaze to make requests, and to share an interest. • Engages other person to help achieve a goal, e.g. to get an object out of reach.
16 to 26 months	• Explores new toys and environments, but 'checks in' regularly with familiar adult as and when needed. • Gradually able to engage in pretend play with toys (supports child to understand their own thinking may be different from others). • Demonstrates sense of self as an individual, e.g. wants to do things independently, says "No" to adult.
22 to 36 months	• Separates from main carer with support and encouragement from a familiar adult. • Expresses own preferences and interests.
30 to 50 months	• Can select and use activities and resources with help. • Welcomes and values praise for what they have done. • Enjoys responsibility of carrying out small tasks. • Is more outgoing towards unfamiliar people and more confident in new social situations.

	• Confident to talk to other children when playing, and will communicate freely about own home and community. • Shows confidence in asking adults for help.
40 to 60+ months	• Confident to speak to others about own needs, wants, interests and opinions. • Can describe self in positive terms and talk about abilities.

Early learning goal – self-confidence and self-awareness

Children are confident to try new activities, and say why they like some activities more than others. They are confident to speak in a familiar group, will talk about their ideas, and will choose the resources they need for their chosen activities. They say when they do or don't need help.

Managing feelings and behaviour

Age	Typical behaviour
Birth to 11 months	• Is comforted by touch and people's faces and voices. • Seeks physical and emotional comfort by snuggling into trusted adults. • Calms from being upset when held, rocked, spoken or sung to with soothing voice. • Shows a range of emotions such as pleasure, fear and excitement. • Reacts emotionally to other people's emotions, e.g. smiles when smiled at and becomes distressed if hears another child crying.
8 to 20 months	• Uses familiar adult to share feelings such as excitement or pleasure, and for 'emotional refuelling' when feeling tired, stressed or frustrated. • Growing ability to soothe themselves, and may like to use a comfort object. • Cooperates with caregiving experiences, e.g. dressing. • Beginning to understand 'yes', 'no' and some boundaries.

16 to 26 months	• Is aware of others' feelings, for example, looks concerned if hears crying or looks excited if hears a familiar happy voice. • Growing sense of will and determination may result in feelings of anger and frustration which are difficult to handle, e.g. may have tantrums. • Responds to a few appropriate boundaries, with encouragement and support. • Begins to learn that some things are theirs, some things are shared, and some things belong to other people.
22 to 36 months	• Seeks comfort from familiar adults when needed. • Can express their own feelings such as sad, happy, cross, scared, worried. • Responds to the feelings and wishes of others. • Aware that some actions can hurt or harm others. • Tries to help or give comfort when others are distressed. • Shows understanding and cooperates with some boundaries and routines. • Can inhibit own actions/behaviours, e.g. stop themselves from doing something they shouldn't do. • Growing ability to distract self when upset, e.g. by engaging in a new play activity.
30 to 50 months	• Aware of own feelings, and knows that some actions and words can hurt others' feelings. • Begins to accept the needs of others and can take turns and share resources, sometimes with support from others. • Can usually tolerate delay when needs are not immediately met, and understands wishes may not always be met. • Can usually adapt behaviour to different events, social situations and changes in routine.
40 to 60+ months	• Understands that own actions affect other people, for example, becomes upset or tries to comfort another child when they realise they have upset them. • Aware of the boundaries set, and of behavioural expectations in the setting. • Beginning to be able to negotiate and solve problems without aggression, e.g. when someone has taken their toy.

Early learning goal – managing feelings and behaviour

Children talk about how they and others show feelings, talk about their own and others' behaviour, and its consequences, and know that some behaviour is unacceptable. They work as part of a group or class, and understand and follow the rules. They adjust their behaviour to different situations, and take changes of routine in their stride.

Making relationships

Age	Typical behaviour
Birth to 11 months	<ul><li>Enjoys the company of others and seeks contact with others from birth.</li><li>Gazes at faces and copies facial movements, e.g. sticking out tongue, opening mouth and widening eyes.</li><li>Responds when talked to, for example, moves arms and legs, changes facial expression, moves body and makes mouth movements.</li><li>Recognises and is most responsive to main carer's voice: face brightens, activity increases when familiar carer appears.</li><li>Responds to what carer is paying attention to, e.g. following their gaze.</li><li>Likes cuddles and being held: calms, snuggles in, smiles, gazes at carer's face or strokes carer's skin.</li></ul>
8 to 20 months	<ul><li>Seeks to gain attention in a variety of ways, drawing others into social interaction.</li><li>Builds relationships with special people.</li><li>Is wary of unfamiliar people.</li><li>Interacts with others and explores new situations when supported by familiar person.</li><li>Shows interest in the activities of others and responds differently to children and adults, e.g. may be more interested in watching children than adults or may pay more attention when children talk to them.</li></ul>

16 to 26 months	<ul><li>Plays alongside others.</li><li>Uses a familiar adult as a secure base from which to explore independently in new environments, e.g. ventures away to play and interact with others, but returns for a cuddle or reassurance if becomes anxious.</li><li>Plays cooperatively with a familiar adult, e.g. rolling a ball back and forth.</li></ul>
22 to 36 months	<ul><li>Interested in others' play and starting to join in.</li><li>Seeks out others to share experiences.</li><li>Shows affection and concern for people who are special to them.</li><li>May form a special friendship with another child.</li></ul>
30 to 50 months	<ul><li>Can play in a group, extending and elaborating play ideas, e.g. building up a role-play activity with other children.</li><li>Initiates play, offering cues to peers to join them.</li><li>Keeps play going by responding to what others are saying or doing.</li><li>Demonstrates friendly behaviour, initiating conversations and forming good relationships with peers and familiar adults.</li></ul>
40 60+ months	<ul><li>Initiates conversations, attends to and takes account of what others say.</li><li>Explains own knowledge and understanding, and asks appropriate questions of others.</li><li>Takes steps to resolve conflicts with other children, e.g. finding a compromise.</li></ul>

Early learning goal – making relationships

Children play co-operatively, taking turns with others. They take account of one another's ideas about how to organise their activity. They show sensitivity to others' needs and feelings, and form positive relationships with adults and other children.

4.   Literacy

The tables below set out what you should be observing a child doing at each stage, if they are developing typically for their age.

Reading

Age	Typical behaviour
Birth to 11 months	• Enjoys looking at books and other printed material with familiar people.
8 to 20 months	• Handles books and printed material with interest.
16 to 26 months	• Interested in books and rhymes and may have favourites.
22 to 36 months	• Has some favourite stories, rhymes, songs, poems or jingles. • Repeats words or phrases from familiar stories. • Fills in the missing word or phrase in a known rhyme, story or game, e.g. 'Humpty Dumpty sat on a …'.
30 to 50 months	• Enjoys rhyming and rhythmic activities. • Shows awareness of rhyme and alliteration. • Recognises rhythm in spoken words. • Listens to and joins in with stories and poems, one-to-one and also in small groups. • Joins in with repeated refrains and anticipates key events and phrases in rhymes and stories. • Beginning to be aware of the way stories are structured. • Suggests how the story might end. • Listens to stories with increasing attention and recall. • Describes main story settings, events and principal characters. • Shows interest in illustrations and print in books and print in the environment. • Recognises familiar words and signs such as own name and advertising logos. • Looks at books independently.

	- Handles books carefully. - Knows information can be relayed in the form of print. - Holds books the correct way up and turns pages. - Knows that print carries meaning and, in English, is read from left to right and top to bottom.
40 to 60+ months	- Continues a rhyming string. - Hears and says the initial sound in words. - Can segment the sounds in simple words and blend them together and knows which letters represent some of them. - Links sounds to letters, naming and sounding the letters of the alphabet. - Begins to read words and simple sentences. - Uses vocabulary and forms of speech that are increasingly influenced by their experiences of books. - Enjoys an increasing range of books. - Knows that information can be retrieved from books and computers.

Early learning goal – reading

Children read and understand simple sentences. They use phonic knowledge to decode regular words and read them aloud accurately. They also read some common irregular words. They demonstrate understanding when talking with others about what they have read.

Writing

Age	Typical behaviour
Birth to 11 months	- Children's later writing is based on skills and understandings which they develop as babies and toddlers. Before they can write, they need to learn to use spoken language to communicate. Later they learn to write down the words they can say.
8 to 20 months	- Early mark-making is not the same as writing. It is a sensory and physical experience for babies and toddlers, which they

16 to 26 months	do not yet connect to forming symbols which can communicate meaning.
22 to 36 months	• Distinguishes between the different marks they make.
30 to 50 months	• Sometimes gives meaning to marks as they draw and paint. • Ascribes meanings to marks that they see in different places
40 to 60+ months	• Gives meaning to marks they make as they draw, write and paint. • Begins to break the flow of speech into words. • Continues a rhyming string. • Hears and says the initial sound in words. • Can segment the sounds in simple words and blend them together. • Links sounds to letters, naming and sounding the letters of the alphabet. • Uses some clearly identifiable letters to communicate meaning, representing some sounds correctly and in sequence. • Writes own name and other things such as labels, captions. • Attempts to write short sentences in meaningful contexts.

Early learning goal – writing

Children use their phonic knowledge to write words in ways which match their spoken sounds. They also write some irregular common words. They write simple sentences which can be read by themselves and others. Some words are spelt correctly and others are phonetically plausible.

5. Mathematics

The tables below set out what you should be observing a child doing at each stage, if they are developing typically for their age.

Numbers

Age	Typical behaviour
Birth to 11 months	• Notices changes in number of objects/images or sounds in group of up to 3.
8 to 20 months	• Develops an awareness of number names through their enjoyment of action rhymes and songs that relate to their experience of numbers. • Has some understanding that things exist, even when out of sight.
16 to 26 months	• Knows that things exist, even when out of sight. • Beginning to organise and categorise objects, e.g. putting all the teddy bears together or teddies and cars in separate piles. • Says some counting words randomly.
22 to 36 months	• Selects a small number of objects from a group when asked, for example, *'please give me one'*, *'please give me two'*. • Recites some number names in sequence. • Creates and experiments with symbols and marks representing ideas of number. • Begins to make comparisons between quantities. • Uses some language of quantities, such as *'more'* and *'a lot'*. • Knows that a group of things changes in quantity when something is added or taken away.
30 to 50 months	• Uses some number names and number language spontaneously. • Uses some number names accurately in play. • Recites numbers in order to 10.

	• Knows that numbers identify how many objects are in a set. • Beginning to represent numbers using fingers, marks on paper or pictures. • Sometimes matches numeral and quantity correctly. • Shows curiosity about numbers by offering comments or asking questions. • Compares two groups of objects, saying when they have the same number. • Shows an interest in number problems. • Separates a group of three or four objects in different ways, beginning to recognise that the total is still the same. • Shows an interest in numerals in the environment. • Shows an interest in representing numbers. • Realises not only objects, but anything can be counted, including steps, claps or jumps.
40 to 60+ months	• Recognise some numerals of personal significance. • Recognises numerals 1 to 5. • Counts up to three or four objects by saying one number name for each item. • Counts actions or objects which cannot be moved. • Counts objects to 10, and beginning to count beyond 10. • Counts out up to six objects from a larger group. • Selects the correct numeral to represent 1 to 5, then 1 to 10 objects. • Counts an irregular arrangement of up to ten objects. • Estimates how many objects they can see and checks by counting them. • Uses the language of 'more' and 'fewer' to compare two sets of objects. • Finds the total number of items in two groups by counting all of them. • Says the number that is one more than a given number. • Finds one more or one less from a group of up to five objects, then ten objects. • In practical activities and discussion, beginning to use the vocabulary involved in adding and subtracting. • Records, using marks that they can interpret and explain. • Begins to identify own mathematical problems based on own interests and fascinations.

Early learning goal – numbers

Children count reliably with numbers from one to 20, place them in order and say which number is one more or one less than a given number. Using quantities and objects, they add and subtract two single-digit numbers and count on or back to find the answer. They solve problems, including doubling, halving and sharing.

Shape, space and measures

Age	Typical behaviour
Birth to 11 months	• Babies' early awareness of shape, space and measure grows from their sensory awareness and opportunities to observe objects and their movements, and to play and explore.
8 to 20 months	• Recognises big things and small things in meaningful contexts. • Gets to know and enjoy daily routines, such as getting-up time, mealtimes, nappy time, and bedtime.
16 to 26 months	• Attempts, sometimes successfully, to fit shapes into spaces on inset boards or jigsaw puzzles. • Uses blocks to create their own simple structures and arrangements. • Enjoys filling and emptying containers. • Associates a sequence of actions with daily routines. • Beginning to understand that things might happen 'now'.
22 to 36 months	• Notices simple shapes and patterns in pictures. • Beginning to categorise objects according to properties such as shape or size. • Begins to use the language of size. • Understands some talk about immediate past and future, e.g. 'before', 'later' or 'soon'. • Anticipates specific time-based events such as mealtimes or home time.

30 to 50 months	• Shows an interest in shape and space by playing with shapes or making arrangements with objects. • Shows awareness of similarities of shapes in the environment. • Uses positional language. • Shows interest in shape by sustained construction activity or by talking about shapes or arrangements. • Shows interest in shapes in the environment. • Uses shapes appropriately for tasks. • Beginning to talk about the shapes of everyday objects, • e.g. '*round*' and '*tall*'.
40 to 60+ months	• Beginning to use mathematical names for 'solid' 3D shapes and 'flat' 2-D shapes, and mathematical terms to describe shapes. • Selects a particular named shape. • Can describe their relative position such as '*behind*' or '*next to*'. • Orders two or three items by length or height. • Orders two items by weight or capacity. • Uses familiar objects and common shapes to create and recreate patterns and build models. • Uses everyday language related to time. • Beginning to use everyday language related to money. • Orders and sequences familiar events. • Measures short periods of time in simple ways.

Early learning goal – shape, space and measures

Children use everyday language to talk about size, weight, capacity, position, distance, time and money to compare quantities and objects and to solve problems. They recognise, create and describe patterns. They explore characteristics of everyday objects and shapes and use mathematical language to describe them.

6. Understanding the world

The tables below set out what you should be observing a child doing at each stage, if they are developing typically for their age.

People and communities

Age	Typical behaviour
Birth to 11 months **8 to 20 months**	• The beginnings of understanding of people and communities lie in early attachment and other relationships.
16 to 26 months	• Is curious about people and shows interest in stories about themselves and their family. • Enjoys pictures and stories about themselves, their families and other people.
22 to 36 months	• Has a sense of own immediate family and relations. • In pretend play, imitates everyday actions and events from own family and cultural background, e.g. making and drinking tea. • Beginning to have their own friends. • Learns that they have similarities and differences that connect them to, and distinguish them from, others.
30 to 50 months	• Shows interest in the lives of people who are familiar to them. • Remembers and talks about significant events in their own experiences. • Recognises and describes special times or events for family or friends. • Shows interest in different occupations and ways of life. • Knows some of the things that make them unique, and can talk about some of the similarities and differences in relation to friends or family.
40 to 60+ months	• Enjoys joining in with family customs and routines.

Early learning goal – people and communities

Children talk about past and present events in their own lives and in the lives of family members. They know that other children don't always enjoy the same things, and are sensitive to this. They know about similarities and differences between themselves and others, and among families, communities and traditions.

The world

Age	Typical behaviour
Birth to 11 months	• Moves eyes, then head, to follow moving objects. • Reacts with abrupt change when a face or object suddenly disappears from view. • Looks around a room with interest; visually scans environment for novel, interesting objects and events. • Smiles with pleasure at recognisable playthings. • Repeats actions that have an effect, e.g. kicking or hitting a mobile or shaking a rattle.
8 to 20 months	• Closely observes what animals, people and vehicles do. • Watches toy being hidden and tries to find it. • Looks for dropped objects. • Becomes absorbed in combining objects, e.g. banging two objects or placing objects into containers. • Knows things are used in different ways, e.g. a ball for rolling or throwing, a toy car for pushing.
16 to 26 months	• Explores objects by linking together different approaches: shaking, hitting, looking, feeling, tasting, mouthing, pulling, turning and poking. • Remembers where objects belong. • Matches parts of objects that fit together, e.g. puts lid on Teapot.

22 to 36 months	• Enjoys playing with small-world models such as a farm, a garage, or a train track. • Notices detailed features of objects in their environment.
30 to 50 months	• Comments and asks questions about aspects of their familiar world such as the place where they live or the natural world. • Can talk about some of the things they have observed such as plants, animals, natural and found objects. • Talks about why things happen and how things work. • Developing an understanding of growth, decay and changes over time. • Shows care and concern for living things and the environment.
40 to 60+ months	• Looks closely at similarities, differences, patterns and change.

Early learning goal – the world

Children know about similarities and differences in relation to places, objects, materials and living things. They talk about the features of their own immediate environment and how environments might vary from one another. They make observations of animals and plants and explain why some things occur, and talk about changes.

Technology

Age	Typical behaviour
Birth to 11 months	• The beginnings of understanding technology lie in babies exploring and making sense of objects and how they behave.
8 to 20 months	
16 to 26 months	• Anticipates repeated sounds, sights and actions, e.g. when an adult demonstrates an action toy several times. • Shows interest in toys with buttons, flaps and simple mechanisms and beginning to learn to operate them.

22 to 36 months	• Seeks to acquire basic skills in turning on and operating equipment. • Operates mechanical toys, e.g. turns the knob on a wind-up toy or pulls back on a friction car.
30 to 50 months	• Knows how to operate simple equipment. • Shows an interest in technological toys with knobs or pulleys, or real objects. • Shows skill in making toys work by pressing parts or lifting flaps to achieve effects such as sound, movements or new images. • Knows that information can be retrieved from computers.
40 to 60+ months	• Completes a simple program on a computer. • Interacts with age-appropriate computer software.

Early learning goal – technology

Children recognise that a range of technology is used in places such as homes and schools. They select and use technology for particular purposes.

7. Expressive arts and design

The tables below sets out what you should be observing a child doing at each stage if they are developing typically for their age.

Exploring and using media and materials

Age	Typical behaviour
Birth to 11 months	• Babies explore media and materials as part of their exploration of the world around them.
8 to 20 months	• Explores and experiments with a range of media through sensory exploration, and using whole body. • Move their whole bodies to sounds they enjoy, such as music or a regular beat.
16 to 26 months	• Imitates and improvises actions they have observed, e.g. clapping or waving. • Begins to move to music, listen to or join in rhymes or songs. • Notices and is interested in the effects of making movements which leave marks.
22 to 36 months	• Joins in singing favourite songs. • Creates sounds by banging, shaking, tapping or blowing. • Shows an interest in the way musical instruments sound. • Experiments with blocks, colours and marks.
30 to 50 months	• Enjoys joining in with dancing and ring games. • Sings a few familiar songs. • Beginning to move rhythmically. • Imitates movement in response to music. • Taps out simple repeated rhythms. • Explores and learns how sounds can be changed. • Explores colour and how colours can be changed. • Understands that they can use lines to enclose a space, and then begin to use these shapes to represent objects. • Beginning to be interested in and describe the texture of things. • Uses various construction materials. • Beginning to construct, stacking blocks vertically and horizontally, making enclosures and creating spaces.

	• Joins construction pieces together to build and balance. • Realises tools can be used for a purpose.
40 to 60+ months	• Begins to build a repertoire of songs and dances. • Explores the different sounds of instruments. • Explores what happens when they mix colours. • Experiments to create different textures. • Understands that different media can be combined to create new effects. • Manipulates materials to achieve a planned effect. • Constructs with a purpose in mind, using a variety of resources. • Uses simple tools and techniques competently and appropriately. • Selects appropriate resources and adapts work where necessary. • Selects tools and techniques needed to shape, assemble and join materials they are using.

Early learning goal – exploring and using media and materials

Children sing songs, make music and dance, and experiment with ways of changing them. They safely use and explore a variety of materials, tools and techniques, experimenting with colour, design, texture, form and function.

Being imaginative

Age	Typical behaviour
Birth to 11 months	• Babies and toddlers need to explore the world and develop a range of ways to communicate before they can express their own ideas through arts and design.
8 to 20 months	
16 to 26 months	• Expresses self through physical action and sound. • Pretends that one object represents another, especially when objects have characteristics in common.

22 to 36 months	• Beginning to use representation to communicate, e.g. drawing a line and saying 'That's me'. • Beginning to make-believe by pretending.
30 to 50 months	• Developing preferences for forms of expression. • Uses movement to express feelings. • Creates movement in response to music. • Sings to self and makes up simple songs. • Makes up rhythms. • Notices what adults do, imitating what is observed and then doing it spontaneously when the adult is not there. • Engages in imaginative role-play based on own first-hand experiences. • Builds stories around toys, e.g. farm animals needing rescue from an armchair 'cliff'. • Uses available resources to create props to support role-play. • Captures experiences and responses with a range of media, such as music, dance and paint and other materials or words.
40 to 60+ months	• Create simple representations of events, people and objects. • Initiates new combinations of movement and gesture in order to express and respond to feelings, ideas and experiences. • Chooses particular colours to use for a purpose. • Introduces a storyline or narrative into their play. • Plays alongside other children who are engaged in the same theme. • Plays cooperatively as part of a group to develop and act out a narrative.

Early learning goal – being imaginative

Children use what they have learnt about media and materials in original ways, thinking about uses and purposes. They represent their own ideas, thoughts and feelings through design and technology, art, music, dance, role play and stories.

Development Matters in the Early Years Foundation Stage (EYFS)

This non-statutory guidance material supports practitioners in implementing the statutory requirements of the EYFS.

Children develop quickly in the early years, and early years practitioners aim to do all they can to help children have the best possible start in life. Children have a right, spelled out in the United Nations Convention on the Rights of the Child, to provision which enables them to develop their personalities, talents and abilities irrespective of ethnicity, culture or religion, home language, family background, learning difficulties, disabilities or gender. This guidance helps adults to understand and support each individual child's development pathway. Other guidance is provided at **www.foundationyears.org.uk**. The EYFS statutory framework is available on the Foundation Years website as well as the Department for Education website: **www.education.gov.uk/publications**

Early Education would like to acknowledge Helen Moylett and Nancy Stewart, Associates of Early Education for their work in producing this document and is grateful to all the early years practitioners, academics and organisations who generously gave them such helpful support, challenge, advice and feedback during the process.

Children are born ready, able and eager to learn. They actively reach out to interact with other people, and in the world around them. Development is not an automatic process, however. It depends on each unique child having opportunities to interact in positive relationships and enabling environments.

The four themes of the EYFS underpin all the guidance. This document - Development Matters - shows how these themes, and the principles that inform them, work together for children in the EYFS.

A Unique Child + Positive Relationships + Enabling Environments = Learning and Development

Themes

Principles

Practice

A Unique Child

Every child is a unique child who is constantly learning and can be resilient, capable, confident and self-assured.

Practitioners

- understand and observe each child's development and learning, assess progress, plan for next steps
- support babies and children to develop a positive sense of their own identity and culture
- identify any need for additional support
- keep children safe
- value and respect all children and families equally

Positive Relationships

Children learn to be strong and independent through positive relationships.

Positive relationships are

- warm and loving, and foster a sense of belonging
- sensitive and responsive to the child's needs, feelings and interests
- supportive of the child's own efforts and independence
- consistent in setting clear boundaries
- stimulating
- built on key person relationships in early years settings

Enabling Environments

Children learn and develop well in enabling environments, in which their experiences respond to their individual needs and there is a strong partnership between practitioners and parents and carers.

Enabling Environments

- value all people
- value learning

They offer

- stimulating resources, relevant to all the children's cultures and communities
- rich learning opportunities through play and playful teaching
- support for children to take risks and explore

Learning and Development

Children develop and learn in different ways. The framework covers the education and care of all children in early years provision, including children with special educational needs and disabilities.

Practitioners teach children by ensuring challenging, playful opportunities across the prime and specific areas of learning and development.

They foster the characteristics of effective early learning

- Playing and exploring
- Active learning
- Creating and thinking critically

Using this guidance to support each child's learning and development

Development matters can help practitioners to support children's learning and development, by closely matching what they provide to a child's current needs.

On-going **formative assessment** is at the heart of effective early years practice. Practitioners can:

- Observe children as they act and interact in their play, everyday activities and planned activities, and learn from parents about what the child does at home **(observation)**.

- Consider the examples of development in the columns headed 'Unique Child: observing what children can do' to help identify where the child may be in their own developmental pathway **(assessment)**.

- Consider ways to support the child to strengthen and deepen their current learning and development, reflecting on guidance in columns headed 'Positive Relationships' and 'Enabling Environments' **(planning)**. These columns contain some examples of what practitioners might do to support learning. Practitioners will develop many other approaches in response to the children with whom they work.

- Where appropriate, use the development statements to identify possible areas in which to challenge and extend the child's current learning and development **(planning)**.

This way of teaching is particularly appropriate to support learning in early years settings.

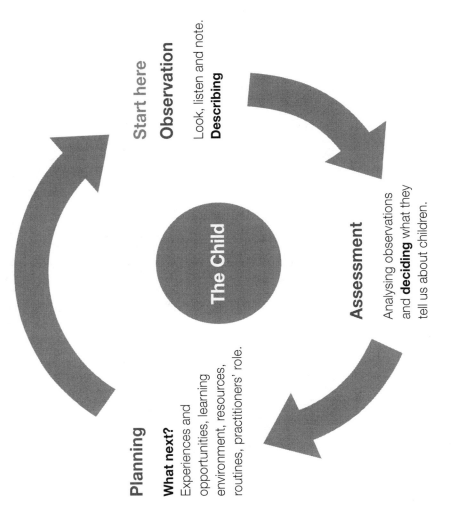

Start here

Observation

Look, listen and note. **Describing**

Planning

What next?
Experiences and opportunities, learning environment, resources, routines, practitioners' role.

The Child

Assessment

Analysing observations and **deciding** what they tell us about children.

Summative assessment

The EYFS requires early years practitioners to review children's progress and share a summary with parents at two points:

- in the prime areas between the ages of 24 and 36 months

- and at the end of the EYFS in the EYFS Profile.

Development Matters might be used by early years settings throughout the EYFS as a guide to making best-fit judgements about whether a child is showing typical development for their age, may be at risk of delay or is ahead for their age. Summative assessment supports information sharing with parents, colleagues and other settings.

The Characteristics of Effective Learning and the prime and specific Areas of Learning and Development are all interconnected.

- The ways in which the child engages with other people and their environment – playing and exploring, active learning, and creating and thinking critically – underpin learning and development across all areas and support the child to remain an effective and motivated learner.

- The **prime** areas begin to develop quickly in response to relationships and experiences, and run through and support learning in all other areas. The prime areas continue to be fundamental throughout the EYFS.

- The **specific** areas include essential skills and knowledge. They grow out of the prime areas, and provide important contexts for learning.

Prime areas are fundamental, work together, and move through to support development in all other areas.

- Personal, Social and Emotional Development
- Communication and Language
- Physical Development

Specific areas include essential skills and knowledge for children to participate successfully in society.

- Literacy
- Mathematics
- Understanding the World
- Expressive Arts and Design

The Unique Child reaches out to relate to people and things through the **Characteristics of Effective Learning**, which move through all areas of learning.

- playing and exploring
- active learning
- creating and thinking critically

Children develop in the context of relationships and the environment around them.

This is unique to each family, and reflects individual communities and cultures.

Area of Learning and Development / Aspect

Area of Learning and Development	Aspect
Prime Areas	
Personal, Social and Emotional Development	Making relationships
	Self-confidence and self-awareness
	Managing feelings and behaviour
Physical Development	Moving and handling
	Health and self-care
Communication and Language	Listening and attention
	Understanding
	Speaking
Specific areas	
Literacy	Reading
	Writing
Mathematics	Numbers
	Shape, space and measure
Understanding the World	People and communities
	The world
	Technology
Expressive Arts and Design	Exploring and using media and materials
	Being imaginative

Characteristics of Effective Learning

Playing and exploring – engagement

Finding out and exploring
Playing with what they know
Being willing to 'have a go'

Active learning – motivation

Being involved and concentrating
Keeping trying
Enjoying achieving what they set out to do

Creating and thinking critically – thinking

Having their own ideas
Making links
Choosing ways to do things

Playing and Exploring, Active Learning, and Creating and Thinking Critically support children's learning across all areas

Characteristics of Effective Learning

	A Unique Child: observing how a child is learning	Positive Relationships: what adults could do	Enabling Environments: what adults could provide
Playing and Exploring *engagement*	**Finding out and exploring** • Showing curiosity about objects, events and people • Using senses to explore the world around them • Engaging in open-ended activity • Showing particular interests **Playing with what they know** • Pretending objects are things from their experience • Representing their experiences in play • Taking on a role in their play • Acting out experiences with other people **Being willing to 'have a go'** • Initiating activities • Seeking challenge • Showing a 'can do' attitude • Taking a risk, engaging in new experiences, and learning by trial and error	• Play with children. Encourage them to explore, and show your own interest in discovering new things. • Help children as needed to do what they are trying to do, without taking over or directing. • Join in play sensitively, fitting in with children's ideas. • Model pretending an object is something else, and help develop roles and stories. • Encourage children to try new activities and to judge risks for themselves. Be sure to support children's confidence with words and body language. • Pay attention to how children engage in activities -- the challenges faced, the effort, thought, learning and enjoyment. Talk more about the process than products. • Talk about how you and the children get better at things through effort and practice, and what we all can learn when things go wrong.	• Provide stimulating resources which are accessible and open-ended so they can be used, moved and combined in a variety of ways. • Make sure resources are relevant to children's interests. • Arrange flexible indoor and outdoor space and resources where children can explore, build, move and role play. • Help children concentrate by limiting noise, and making spaces visually calm and orderly. • Plan first-hand experiences and challenges appropriate to the development of the children. • Ensure children have uninterrupted time to play and explore.
	A Unique Child: observing how a child is learning	Positive Relationships: what adults could do	Enabling Environments: what adults could provide
Active Learning *motivation*	**Being involved and concentrating** • Maintaining focus on their activity for a period of time • Showing high levels of energy, fascination • Not easily distracted • Paying attention to details **Keeping on trying** • Persisting with activity when challenges occur • Showing a belief that more effort or a different approach will pay off • Bouncing back after difficulties **Enjoying achieving what they set out to do** • Showing satisfaction in meeting their own goals • Being proud of how they accomplished something – not just the end result • Enjoying meeting challenges for their own sake rather than external rewards or praise	• Support children to choose their activities – what they want to do and how they will do it. • Stimulate children's interest through shared attention, and calm over-stimulated children. • Help children to become aware of their own goals, make plans, and to review their own progress and successes. Describe what you see them trying to do, and encourage children to talk about their own processes and successes. • Be specific when you praise, especially noting effort such as how the child concentrates, tries different approaches, persists, solves problems, and has new ideas. • Encourage children to learn together and from each other. • Children develop their own motivations when you give reasons and talk about learning, rather than just directing.	• Children will become more deeply involved when you provide something that is new and unusual for them to explore, especially when it is linked to their interests. • Notice what arouses children's curiosity, looking for signs of deep involvement to identify learning that is intrinsically motivated. • Ensure children have time and freedom to become deeply involved in activities. • Children can maintain focus on things that interest them over a period of time. Help them to keep ideas in mind by talking over photographs of their previous activities. • Keep significant activities out instead of routinely tidying them away. • Make space and time for all children to contribute.

Children develop at their own rates, and in their own ways. The development statements and their order should not be taken as necessary steps for individual children. They should not be used as checklists. The age/stage bands overlap because these are not fixed age boundaries but suggest a typical range of development.

Playing and Exploring, Active Learning, and Creating and Thinking Critically support children's learning across all areas

Characteristics of Effective Learning

	A Unique Child: observing how a child is learning	Positive Relationships: what adults could do	Enabling Environments: what adults could provide
Creating and Thinking Critically *thinking*	**Having their own ideas** • Thinking of ideas • Finding ways to solve problems • Finding new ways to do things **Making links** • Making links and noticing patterns in their experience • Making predictions • Testing their ideas • Developing ideas of grouping, sequences, cause and effect **Choosing ways to do things** • Planning, making decisions about how to approach a task, solve a problem and reach a goal • Checking how well their activities are going • Changing strategy as needed • Reviewing how well the approach worked	• Use the language of thinking and learning: *think, know, remember, forget, idea, makes sense, plan, learn, find out, confused, figure out, trying to do.* • Model being a thinker, showing that you don't always know, are curious and sometimes puzzled, and can think and find out. • Encourage open-ended thinking by not settling on the first ideas: *What else is possible?* • Always respect children's efforts and ideas, so they feel safe to take a risk with a new idea. • Talking aloud helps children to think and control what they do. Model self-talk, describing your actions in play. • Give children time to talk and think. • Value questions, talk, and many possible responses, without rushing toward answers too quickly. • Support children's interests over time, reminding them of previous approaches and encouraging them to make connections between their experiences. • Model the creative process, showing your thinking about some of the many possible ways forward. • Sustained shared thinking helps children to explore ideas and make links. Follow children's lead in conversation, and think about things together. • Encourage children to describe problems they encounter, and to suggest ways to solve the problem. • Show and talk about strategies – how to do things – including problem-solving, thinking and learning. • Give feedback and help children to review their own progress and learning. Talk with children about what they are doing, how they plan to do it, what worked well and what they would change next time. • Model the plan-do-review process yourself.	• In planning activities, ask yourself: *Is this an opportunity for children to find their own ways to represent and develop their own ideas?* Avoid children just reproducing someone else's ideas. • Build in opportunities for children to play with materials before using them in planned tasks. • Play is a key opportunity for children to think creatively and flexibly, solve problems and link ideas. Establish the enabling conditions for rich play: space, time, flexible resources, choice, control, warm and supportive relationships. • Recognisable and predictable routines help children to predict and make connections in their experiences. • Routines can be flexible, while still basically orderly. • Plan linked experiences that follow the ideas children are really thinking about. • Use mind-maps to represent thinking together. • Develop a learning community which focuses on **how** and not just what we are learning.

Children develop at their own rates, and in their own ways. The development statements and their order should not be taken as necessary steps for individual children. They should not be used as checklists. The age/stage bands overlap because these are not fixed age boundaries but suggest a typical range of development.

Playing and Exploring, Active Learning, and Creating and Thinking Critically support children's learning across all areas

Personal, Social and Emotional Development: Making relationships

	A Unique Child: observing what a child is learning	Positive Relationships: what adults could do	Enabling Environments: what adults could provide
Birth – 11 months	• Enjoys the company of others and seeks contact with others from birth. • Gazes at faces and copies facial movements. e.g. sticking out tongue, opening mouth and widening eyes. • Responds when talked to, for example, moves arms and legs, changes facial expression, moves body and makes mouth movements. • Recognises and is most responsive to main carer's voice: face brightens, activity increases when familiar carer appears. • Responds to what carer is paying attention to, e.g. following their gaze. • Likes cuddles and being held: calms, snuggles in, smiles, gazes at carer's face or strokes carer's skin.	• Make sure babies have their own special person in the setting, who knows them really well and understands their wants and needs. • Tune in sensitively to babies, and provide warm, loving, consistent care, responding quickly to babies' needs. • Hold and handle babies, since sensitive touch helps to build security and attachment. • Ensure that the key person or buddy is available to greet a young baby at the beginning of the session, and to hand them over to parents at the end of a session, so the young baby is supported and communication with parents is maintained. • Engage in playful interactions that encourage young babies to respond to, or mimic, adults. • Follow the baby's lead by repeating vocalisations, mirroring movements and showing the baby that you are 'listening' fully. • Notice when babies turn away, signalling their need for less stimulation. • Discover from parents the copying games that their babies enjoy, and use these as the basis for your play. • Talk with babies about special people, such as their family members, e.g. grandparents.	• Ensure staff are aware of the importance of attachment in relationships. • Ensure the key person is paired with a 'buddy' who knows the baby and family as well, and can step in when necessary. • At times of transition (such as shift changes) make sure staff greet and say goodbye to babies and their carers. This helps to develop secure and trusting three-way relationships. • Plan to have one-to-one time to interact with young babies when they are in an alert and responsive state and willing to engage. • Display photos of family and other special people. • Share knowledge about languages with staff and parents and make a poster or book of greetings in all languages used within the setting and the community. • Repeat greetings at the start and end of each session, so that young babies recognise and become familiar with these daily rituals.
8-20 months	• Seeks to gain attention in a variety of ways, drawing others into social interaction. • Builds relationships with special people. • Is wary of unfamiliar people. • Interacts with others and explores new situations when supported by familiar person. • Shows interest in the activities of others and responds differently to children and adults, e.g. may be more interested in watching children than adults or may pay more attention when children talk to them.		
16-26 months	• Plays alongside others. • Uses a familiar adult as a secure base from which to explore independently in new environments, e.g. ventures away to play and interact with others, but returns for a cuddle or reassurance if becomes anxious. • Plays cooperatively with a familiar adult, e.g. rolling a ball back and forth.	• Involve all children in welcoming and caring for one another. • Give your full attention when young children look to you for a response. • Enable children to explore by providing a secure base for them. • Help young children to understand the feelings of others by labelling emotions such as sadness or happiness.	• Play name games to welcome children to the setting and help them get to know each other and the staff. • Regularly evaluate the way you respond to different children. • Ensure there are opportunities for the child to play alongside others and play cooperative games with a familiar adult. • Provide matching items to encourage adult and child to mimic each other in a cooperative game. e.g. two identical musical instruments.

Children develop at their own rates, and in their own ways. The development statements and their order should not be taken as necessary steps for individual children. They should not be used as checklists. The age/stage bands overlap because these are not fixed are boundaries but suggest a typical range of development...

Playing and Exploring, Active Learning, and Creating and Thinking Critically support children's learning across all areas

Personal, Social and Emotional Development: Making relationships

		A Unique Child: observing what a child is learning	Positive Relationships: what adults could do	Enabling Environments: what adults could provide
22-36 months		• Interested in others' play and starting to join in. • Seeks out others to share experiences. • Shows affection and concern for people who are special to them. • May form a special friendship with another child.	• Ensure that children have opportunities to join in. • Help them to recognise and understand the rules for being together with others, such as waiting for a turn. • Continue to talk about feelings such as sadness, happiness, or feeling cross. • Model ways of noticing how others are feeling and comforting/helping them.	• Make time for children to be with their key person, individually and in their key group. • Create areas in which children can sit and chat with friends, such as a snug den and cosy spaces. • Provide resources that promote cooperation between two children such as a big ball to roll or throw to each other.
30-50 months		• Can play in a group, extending and elaborating play ideas, e.g. building up a role-play activity with other children. • Initiates play, offering cues to peers to join them. • Keeps play going by responding to what others are saying or doing. • Demonstrates friendly behaviour, initiating conversations and forming good relationships with peers and familiar adults.	• Support children in developing positive relationships by challenging negative comments and actions towards either peers or adults. • Encourage children to choose to play with a variety of friends from all backgrounds, so that everybody in the group experiences being included. • Help children understand the feelings of others by labelling emotions such as sadness, happiness, feeling cross, lonely, scared or worried. • Plan support for children who have not yet made friends.	• Plan activities that require collaboration, such as parachute activities and ring games. • Provide stability in staffing, key person relationships and in grouping of the children. • Provide time, space and materials for children to collaborate with one another in different ways, for example, building constructions. • Provide a role-play area resourced with materials reflecting children's family lives and communities. Consider including resources reflecting lives that are unfamiliar, to broaden children's knowledge and reflect an inclusive ethos. • Choose books, puppets and dolls that help children explore their ideas about friends and friendship and to talk about feelings, e.g. someone saying 'You can't play'.
40-60+ months		• Initiates conversations, attends to and takes account of what others say. • Explains own knowledge and understanding, and asks appropriate questions of others. • Takes steps to resolve conflicts with other children, e.g. finding a compromise. **Early Learning Goal** **Children play co-operatively, taking turns with others. They take account of one another's ideas about how to organise their activity. They show sensitivity to others' needs and feelings, and form positive relationships with adults and other children.**	• Support children in linking openly and confidently with others, e.g. to seek help or check information. • Model being a considerate and responsive partner in interactions. • Ensure that children and adults make opportunities to listen to each other and explain their actions. • Be aware of and respond to particular needs of children who are learning English as an additional language.	• Ensure that children have opportunities over time to get to know everyone in the group, not just their special friends. • Ensure children have opportunities to relate to their key person, individually and in small groups. • Provide activities that involve turn-taking and sharing in small groups.

Children develop at their own rates, and in their own ways. The development statements and their order should not be taken as necessary steps for individual children. They should not be used as checklists. The age/stage bands overlap because these are not fixed age boundaries but suggest a typical range of development.

Playing and Exploring, Active Learning, and Creating and Thinking Critically support children's learning across all areas

Personal, Social and Emotional Development: Self-confidence and self-awareness

	A Unique Child: observing what a child is learning	Positive Relationships: what adults could do	Enabling Environments: what adults could provide
Birth - 11 months	• Laughs and gurgles, e.g. shows pleasure at being tickled and other physical interactions. • Uses voice, gesture, eye contact and facial expression to make contact with people and keep their attention.	• Show your pleasure in being with the baby. • Be close by and available, to ensure that babies feel safe and loved even when they are not the centre of adult attention. • Say or sing made-up rhymes or songs while stroking or pointing to the babies' hands, feet or cheeks. • Respond to and build on babies' expressions, actions, and gestures. Babies will repeat actions that get a positive response from you. • Find out what babies like and dislike through talking to their parents.	• Provide a sofa or comfy chair so that parents, practitioners and young babies can sit together. • Give babies toys to hold while you are preparing their food, or gathering materials for a nappy change. • Plan to have times when babies and older siblings or friends can be together. • Devote uninterrupted time to babies when you can play with them when they are ready to engage. Be attentive and fully focused. • Plan time to share and reflect with parents on babies' progress and development, ensuring appropriate support is available where parents do not speak or understand English.
8-20 months	• Enjoys finding own nose, eyes or tummy as part of naming games. • Learns that own voice and actions have effects on others. • Uses pointing with eye gaze to make requests, and to share an interest. • Engages other person to help achieve a goal, e.g: to get an object out of reach.	• Playfully help babies to recognise that they are separate and different from others, e.g. pointing to own and baby's nose, eyes, fingers. • Give opportunities for babies to have choice, where possible. • Follow young babies' lead as they explore their surroundings, people and resources. • Talk to babies about puzzles they encounter such as how to get their sock back from where it has fallen, asking whether they can do it or if they might need help.	• Place mirrors where babies can see their own reflection. Talk with them about what they see. • Offer choices, e.g. different vegetables and fruit at snack time or different toys. • Allow enough space for babies to move, roll, stretch and explore. • Respond to what babies show you they are interested in and want to do, by providing a variety of activities, stories and games.
16-26 months	• Explores new toys and environments, but 'checks in' regularly with familiar adult as and when needed. • Gradually able to engage in pretend play with toys (supports child to understand their own thinking may be different from others). • Demonstrates sense of self as an individual, e.g. wants to do things independently, says "No" to adult.	• Make sure the child can explore from the secure, close-by presence of their key person. • Model pretend play. • Share children's pleasure when they do something for themselves.	• Making choices is important for all children. Consider ways in which you provide for children with disabilities to make choices, and express preferences about their carers and activities. • Display photographs of carers, so that when young children arrive, their parents can show them who will be there to take care of them. • Share with children photographs of their activities, talking with them about what they did and how they felt.

Children develop at their own rates, and in their own ways. The development statements and their order should not be taken as necessary steps for individual children. They should not be used as checklists. The age/stage bands overlap because these are not fixed age boundaries but suggest a typical range of development.

Playing and Exploring, Active Learning, and Creating and Thinking Critically support children's learning across all areas

Personal, Social and Emotional Development: Self-confidence and self-awareness

Age	A Unique Child: observing what a child is learning	Positive Relationships: what adults could do	Enabling Environments: what adults could provide
22-36 months	• Separates from main carer with support and encouragement from a familiar adult. • Expresses own preferences and interests.	• Recognise that children's interest may last for short or long periods, and that their interest and preferences vary. • Value and support the decisions that children make • Talk to children about choices they have made, and help them understand that this may mean that they cannot do something else. • Be aware of cultural differences in attitudes and expectations. Continue to share and explain practice with parents, ensuring a two-way communication using interpreter support where necessary.	• Discuss with staff and parents how each child responds to activities, adults and their peers. • Build on this to plan future activities and experiences for each child. • As children differ in their degree of self-assurance, plan to convey to each child that you appreciate them and their efforts. • Consult with parents about children's varying levels of confidence in different situations. • Record individual achievements which reflect significant progress for every child.
30-50 months	• Can select and use activities and resources with help. • Welcomes and values praise for what they have done. • Enjoys responsibility of carrying out small tasks. • Is more outgoing towards unfamiliar people and more confident in new social situations. • Confident to talk to other children when playing, and will communicate freely about own home and community. • Shows confidence in asking adults for help.	• Encourage children to see adults as a resource and as partners in their learning. • Teach children to use and care for materials, and then trust them to do so independently. • Ensure that key practitioners offer extra support to children in new situations.	• Seek and exchange information with parents about young children's concerns, so that they can be reassured if they feel uncertain. • Vary activities so that children are introduced to different materials. • Make materials easily accessible at child height, to ensure everybody can make choices.
40-60+ months	• Confident to speak to others about own needs, wants, interests and opinions. • Can describe self in positive terms and talk about abilities. **Early Learning Goal** **Children are confident to try new activities, and say why they like some activities more than others. They are confident to speak in a familiar group, will talk about their ideas, and will choose the resources they need for their chosen activities. They say when they do or don't need help.**	• Encourage children to explore and talk about what they are learning, valuing their ideas and ways of doing things. • Offer help with activities when asked but not before. • Intervene when children need help with difficult situations, e.g. is experiencing prejudice or unkindness. • Recognising and enjoying children's success with them helps them to feel confident. • Support children to feel good about their own success, rather than relying on a judgement from you such as wanting a sticker.	• Give time for children to pursue their learning without interruption, to complete activities to their satisfaction, and to return to activities. • Provide experiences and activities that are challenging but achievable. • Provide opportunities for children to reflect on successes, achievements and their own gifts and talents. • Provide regular opportunities for children to talk to their small group about something they are interested in or have done. • Involve children in drawing or taking photographs of favourite activities or places, to help them describe their individual preferences and opinions.

Children develop at their own rates, and in their own ways. The development statements and their order should not be taken as necessary steps for individual children. They should not be used as checklists. The age/stage bands overlap because these are not fixed age boundaries but suggest a typical range of development.

Playing and Exploring, Active Learning, and Creating and Thinking Critically support children's learning across all areas

Personal, Social and Emotional Development: Managing feelings and behaviour

	A Unique Child: observing what a child is learning	Positive Relationships: what adults could do	Enabling Environments: what adults could provide
Birth - 11 months	• Is comforted by touch and people's faces and voices. • Seeks physical and emotional comfort by snuggling in to trusted adults. • Calms from being upset when held, rocked, spoken or sung to with soothing voice. • Shows a range of emotions such as pleasure, fear and excitement. • Reacts emotionally to other people's emotions, e.g. smiles when smiled at and becomes distressed if hears another child crying.	• Find out as much as you can from parents about young babies before they join the setting, so that the routines you follow are familiar and comforting. • Use calming processes such as rocking or hugging.	• Learn lullabies that children know from home and share them with others in the setting. • Have a cosy, quiet place for babies to be calm. • Provide comfortable seating such as a sofa or cushions for baby and key person to be together. • Suggest to parents bringing something from home as a transitional (comfort) object.
8-20 months	• Uses familiar adult to share feelings such as excitement or pleasure, and for 'emotional refuelling' when feeling tired, stressed or frustrated. • Growing ability to soothe themselves, and may like to use a comfort object. • Cooperates with caregiving experiences, e.g. dressing. • Beginning to understand 'yes', 'no' and some boundaries.	• Establish shared understandings between home and setting about ways of responding to babies' emotions. • Make sure the key person stays close by and provides a secure presence and a refuge at times a child may be feeling anxious. • Support children who are anxious on separating from their parents by acknowledging their feelings and reassuring them. • Demonstrate clear and consistent boundaries and reasonable yet challenging expectations.	• Have resources including picture books and stories that focus on a range of emotions, such as 'I am happy'. • Keep toys and comforters in areas that are easy for babies to locate. • Ensure that children can use their comfort objects from home when in the setting. • Share information with parents to create consistency between home and setting so that babies learn about boundaries.
16-26 months	• Is aware of others' feelings, for example, looks concerned if hears crying or looks excited if hears a familiar happy voice. • Growing sense of will and determination may result in feelings of anger and frustration which are difficult to handle, e.g. may have tantrums. • Responds to a few appropriate boundaries, with encouragement and support. • Begins to learn that some things are theirs, some things are shared, and some things belong to other people.	• Help young children to label emotions such as sadness or happiness, by talking to them about their own feelings and those of others. • Be aware of and alert to possible dangers, while recognising the importance of encouraging young children's sense of exploration and risk-taking. • Reduce incidents of frustration and conflict by keeping routines flexible so that young children can pursue their interests.	• Choose books and stories in which characters help and support each other. • Duplicate some materials and resources to reduce conflict, e.g. two tricycles or two copies of the same book.

Children develop at their own rates, and in their own ways. The development statements and their order should not be taken as necessary steps for individual children. They should not be used as checklists. The age/stage bands overlap because these are not fixed age boundaries but suggest a typical range of development.

Playing and Exploring, Active Learning, and Creating and Thinking Critically support children's learning across all areas

Personal, Social and Emotional Development: Managing feelings and behaviour

	A Unique Child: observing what a child is learning	Positive Relationships: what adults could do	Enabling Environments: what adults could provide
22-36 months	• Seeks comfort from familiar adults when needed. • Can express their own feelings such as sad, happy, cross, scared, worried. • Responds to the feelings and wishes of others. • Aware that some actions can hurt or harm others. • Tries to help or give comfort when others are distressed. • Shows understanding and cooperates with some boundaries and routines. • Can inhibit own actions/behaviours, e.g. stop themselves from doing something they shouldn't do. • Growing ability to distract self when upset, e.g. by engaging in a new play activity.	• Support children's symbolic play, recognising that pretending to do something can help a child to express their feelings. • Help children to understand their rights to be kept safe by others, and encourage them to talk about ways to avoid harming or hurting others. • Help children to recognise when their actions hurt others. Be wary of expecting children to say 'sorry' before they have a real understanding of what this means.	• Have agreed procedures outlining how to respond to changes in children's behaviour. • Share policies and practice with parents, ensuring an accurate two-way exchange of information through an interpreter or through translated materials, where necessary. • Provide areas to mirror different moods and feelings- quiet restful areas as well as areas for active exploration. • Provide books, stories, puppets that can be used to model responding to others' feelings and being helpful and supportive to them.
30-50 months	• Aware of own feelings, and knows that some actions and words can hurt others' feelings. • Begins to accept the needs of others and can take turns and share resources, sometimes with support from others. • Can usually tolerate delay when needs are not immediately met, and understands wishes may not always be met. • Can usually adapt behaviour to different events, social situations and changes in routine.	• Name and talk about a wide range of feelings and make it clear that all feelings are understandable and acceptable, including feeling angry, but that not all behaviours are. • Model how you label and manage your own feelings, e.g. 'I'm feeling a bit angry and I need to calm down, so I'm going to…' • Ask children for their ideas on what might make people feel better when they are sad or cross. • Show your own concern and respect for others, living things and the environment. • Establish routines with predictable sequences and events. • Prepare children for changes that may occur in the routine. • Share with parents the rationale of boundaries and expectations to maintain a joint approach. • Model and involve children in finding solutions to problems and conflicts. • Collaborate with children in creating explicit rules for the care of the environment.	• Provide photographs and pictures of emotions for children to look at and talk about. • Use Persona Dolls to help children consider feelings, ways to help others feel better about themselves, and dealing with conflicting opinions. • Make available a range of music that captures different moods. • Put in place ways in which children can let others know how they are feeling, such as pegging their own photo onto a feelings tree or feelings faces washing line. • Provide familiar, predictable routines, including opportunities to help in appropriate tasks, e.g. dusting, setting table or putting away toys. • To support children with SEN, use a sequence of photographs to show children the routines in the setting. • Set, explain and maintain clear, reasonable and consistent limits so that children can feel safe and secure in their play and other activities. • Use pictures or consistent gestures to show children with SEN the expected behaviours. • Provide materials for a variety of role play themes. • Provide a safe space for children to calm down or when they need to be quiet. • Provide activities that help children to develop safe ways of dealing with anger and other strong feelings.

Children develop at their own rates, and in their own ways. The development statements and their order should not be taken as necessary steps for individual children. They should not be used as checklists. The age/stage bands overlap because these are not fixed age boundaries but suggest a typical range of development.

Playing and Exploring, Active Learning, and Creating and Thinking Critically support children's learning across all areas

Personal, Social and Emotional Development: Managing feelings and behaviour

	A Unique Child: observing what a child is learning	Positive Relationships: what adults could do	Enabling Environments: what adults could provide
40-60+ months	• Understands that own actions affect other people, for example, becomes upset or tries to comfort another child when they realise they have upset them. • Aware of the boundaries set, and of behavioural expectations in the setting. • Beginning to be able to negotiate and solve problems without aggression, e.g. when someone has taken their toy. **Early Learning Goal** **Children talk about how they and others show feelings, talk about their own and others' behaviour, and its consequences, and know that some behaviour is unacceptable. They work as part of a group or class, and understand and follow the rules. They adjust their behaviour to different situations, and take changes of routine in their stride.**	• Talk about fair and unfair situations, children's feelings about fairness, and how we can make things fair. • Model being fair, e.g. when choosing children for special jobs. • Be alert to injustices and let children see that they are addressed and resolved. • Affirm and praise positive behaviour, explaining that it makes children and adults feel happier. • Encourage children to think about issues from the viewpoint of others. • Ensure that children have opportunities to identify and discuss boundaries, so that they understand why they are there and what they are intended to achieve. • Make time to listen to children respectfully and kindly, and explain to all the children why this is important. Children will then know that they will be listened to when they raise injustices.	• Plan small group circle times when children can explore feelings, e.g. help children to recall when they were happy, when they were excited, or when they felt lonely. • Provide activities that require give and take or sharing for things to be fair. • Use Persona Dolls to support children in considering fair ways to share and get on with each other. • Involve children in agreeing codes of behaviour and taking responsibility for implementing them. • Provide books with stories about characters that follow or break rules, and the effects of their behaviour on others. • Carefully prepare children with SEN, such as those with autistic spectrum disorder, for any changes to their routine.

Children develop at their own rates, and in their own ways. The development statements and their order should not be taken as necessary steps for individual children. They should not be used as checklists. The age/stage bands overlap because these are not fixed age boundaries but suggest a typical range of development

Playing and Exploring, Active Learning, and Creating and Thinking Critically support children's learning across all areas

Communication and Language: Listening and attention

	A Unique Child: observing what a child is learning	Positive Relationships: what adults could do	Enabling Environments: what adults could provide
Birth - 11 months	• Turns toward a familiar sound then locates range of sounds with accuracy. • Listens to, distinguishes and responds to intonations and sounds of voices. • Reacts in interaction with others by smiling, looking and moving. • Quietens or alerts to the sound of speech. • Looks intently at a person talking, but stops responding if speaker turns away. • Listens to familiar sounds, words, or finger plays. • Fleeting Attention – not under child's control, new stimuli takes whole attention.	• Being physically close, making eye contact, using touch or voice all provide ideal opportunities for early conversations between adults and babies, and between one baby and another. • Encourage playfulness, turn-taking and responses, including peek-a-boo and rhymes. • Use a lively voice, with ups and downs to help babies tune in. • Sing songs and rhymes during everyday routines. • Use repeated sounds, and words and phrases so babies can begin to recognise particular sounds.	• Share stories, songs and rhymes from all cultures and in babies' home languages. • Display photographs showing how young babies communicate. • Share favourite stories as babies are settling to sleep, or at other quiet times. • Plan times when you can sing with young babies, encouraging them to join in. • Create an environment which invites responses from babies and adults, for example, touching, smiling, smelling, feeling, listening, exploring, describing and sharing.
8-20 months	• Moves whole bodies to sounds they enjoy, such as music or a regular beat. • Has a strong exploratory impulse. • Concentrates intently on an object or activity of own choosing for short periods. • Pays attention to dominant stimulus – easily distracted by noises or other people talking.		
16-26 months	• Listens to and enjoys rhythmic patterns in rhymes and stories. • Enjoys rhymes and demonstrates listening by trying to join in with actions or vocalisations. • Rigid attention – may appear not to hear.	• Encourage young children to explore and imitate sound. • Talk about the different sounds they hear, such as a tractor's "chug chug" while sharing a book.	• Collect resources that children can listen to and learn to distinguish between. These may include noises in the street, and games that involve guessing which object makes a particular sound
22-36 months	• Listens with interest to the noises adults make when they read stories. • Recognises and responds to many familiar sounds, e.g. turning to a knock on the door, looking at or going to the door. • Shows interest in play with sounds, songs and rhymes. • Single channelled attention. Can shift to a different task if attention fully obtained – using child's name helps focus.	• Encourage repetition, rhythm and rhyme by using tone and intonation as you tell, recite or sing stories, poems and rhymes from books. • Be aware of the needs of children learning English as an additional language from a variety of cultures and ask parents to share their favourites from their home languages.	• Keep background noise to a minimum, e.g. use music or radio briefly only for particular purposes. • Use puppets and other props to encourage listening and responding when singing a familiar song or reading from a story book. • Encourage children to learn one another's names and to pronounce them correctly. • Ensure all staff can pronounce the names of children, parents and other staff members. Make sure that shortened names and nicknames are not substituted instead.

Children develop at their own rates, and in their own ways. The development statements and their order should not be taken as necessary steps for individual children. They should not be used as checklists. The age/stage bands overlap because these are not fixed age boundaries but suggest a typical range of development.

Playing and Exploring, Active Learning, and Creating and Thinking Critically support children's learning across all areas

Communication and Language: Listening and attention

	A Unique Child: observing what a child is learning	Positive Relationships: what adults could do	Enabling Environments: what adults could provide
30-50 months	• Listens to others one to one or in small groups, when conversation interests them. • Listens to stories with increasing attention and recall. • Joins in with repeated refrains and anticipates key events and phrases in rhymes and stories. • Focusing attention – still listen or do, but can shift own attention. • Is able to follow directions (if not intently focused on own choice of activity).	• Model being a listener by listening to children and taking account of what they say in your responses to them. • Cue children, particularly those with communication difficulties, into a change of conversation, e.g. 'Now we are going to talk about...' • For those children who find it difficult to 'listen and do', say their name before giving an instruction or asking a question. • Share rhymes, books and stories from many cultures, sometimes using languages other than English, particularly where children are learning English as an additional language. Children then all hear a range of languages and recognise the skill needed to speak more than one. • Introduce 'rhyme time' bags containing books to take home and involve parents in rhymes and singing games. • Ask parents to record regional variations of songs and rhymes.	• When making up alliterative jingles, draw attention to the similarities in sounds at the beginning of words and emphasise the initial sound, e.g. "mmmmummy", "shshshshadow," "K-K-K-Katy". • Plan activities listening carefully to different speech sounds, e.g. a sound chain copying the voice sound around the circle, or identifying other children's voices on tape. • Help children be aware of different voice sounds by using a mirror to see what their mouth and tongue do as they make different sounds. • When singing or saying rhymes, talk about the similarities in the rhyming words. Make up alternative endings and encourage children to supply the last word of the second line, e.g. 'Hickory Dickory boot, The mouse ran down the... • Set up a listening area where children can enjoy rhymes and stories.
40-60+ months	• Maintains attention, concentrates and sits quietly during appropriate activity. • Two-channelled attention – can listen and do for short span. **Early Learning Goal** **Children listen attentively in a range of situations. They listen to stories, accurately anticipating key events and respond to what they hear with relevant comments, questions or actions. They give their attention to what others say and respond appropriately, while engaged in another activity.**	• Play games which involve listening for a signal, such as 'Simon Says', and use 'ready, steady...go!' • Use opportunities to stop and listen carefully for environmental sounds, and talk about sounds you can hear such as long, short, high, low. • Explain why it is important to pay attention when others are speaking. • Give children opportunities both to speak and to listen, ensuring that the needs of children learning English as an additional language are met, so that they can participate fully.	• Choose stories with repeated refrains, dances and action songs involving looking and pointing, and songs that require replies and turn-taking such as 'Tommy Thumb'. • Plan regular short periods when individuals listen to others, such as singing a short song, sharing an experience or describing something they have seen or done. • Use sand timers to help extend concentration for children who find it difficult to focus their attention on a task.

Children develop at their own rates, and in their own ways. The development statements and their order should not be taken as necessary steps for individual children. They should not be used as checklists. The age/stage bands overlap because these are not fixed age boundaries but suggest a typical range of development

Playing and Exploring, Active Learning, and Creating and Thinking Critically support children's learning across all areas

Communication and Language: Understanding

	A Unique Child: observing what a child is learning	Positive Relationships: what adults could do	Enabling Environments: what adults could provide
Birth – 11 months	• Stops and looks when hears own name. • Starts to understand contextual clues, e.g. familiar gestures, words and sounds.	• Look at the baby and say their name. Make eye contact and wait for them to react. • Interpret and give meaning to the things young babies show interest in, e.g. when babies point to an object tell them what it is. • Talk to babies about what you are doing and what is happening, so they will link words with actions, e.g. preparing lunch.	• Let babies see and hear the sequence of actions you go through as you carry out familiar routines. • Provide resources that stimulate babies' interests such as a shiny bell, a book or a mirror. • Display lists of words from different home languages, and invite parents and other adults to contribute. Include languages such as Romany and Creole, since seeing their languages reflected in the setting will encourage all parents to feel involved and valued. • When you use nursery rhymes, help children understand the words by using actions as well.
8-20 months	• Developing the ability to follow others' body language, including pointing and gesture. • Responds to the different things said when in a familiar context with a special person (e.g. 'Where's Mummy?', 'Where's your nose?'). • Understanding of single words in context is developing, e.g. 'cup', 'milk', 'daddy'.	• Use actions to support your words, e.g. waving when you say 'bye bye'. • Speak clearly. Babies respond well to a higher pitched, sing-song voice. • Use and repeat single words, so the baby can gradually link the word to its meaning.	• Plan play activities and provide resources which encourage young children to engage in symbolic play, e.g. putting a 'baby' to bed and talking to it appropriately. • Use pictures, books, real objects, and signs alongside your words.
16-26 months	• Selects familiar objects by name and will go and find objects when asked, or identify objects from a group. • Understands simple sentences (e.g. 'Throw the ball.')	• Be aware that young children's understanding is much greater than their ability to express their thoughts and ideas. • Recognise young children's competence and appreciate their efforts when they show their understanding of new words and phrases.	
22-36 months	• Identifies action words by pointing to the right picture, e.g., "Who's jumping?" • Understands more complex sentences, e.g. 'Put your toys away and then we'll read a book.' • Understands 'who', 'what', 'where' in simple questions (e.g. Who's that/can? What's that? Where is.?). • Developing understanding of simple concepts (e.g. big/little).	• Use talk to describe what children are doing by providing a running commentary, e.g. 'Oh, I can see what you are doing. You have to put the milk in the cup first.' • Provide opportunities for children to talk with other children and adults about what they see, hear, think and feel.	• Include things which excite young children's curiosity, such as hats, bubbles, shells, story books, seeds and snails. • Provide activities, such as cooking, where talk is used to anticipate or initiate what children will be doing, e.g. "We need some eggs. Let's see if we can find some in here."

Children develop at their own rates, and in their own ways. The development statements and their order should not be taken as necessary steps for individual children. They should not be used as checklists. The age/stage bands overlap because these are not fixed age boundaries but suggest a typical range of development.

Playing and Exploring, Active Learning, and Creating and Thinking Critically support children's learning across all areas

Communication and Language: Understanding

	A Unique Child: observing what a child is learning	Positive Relationships: what adults could do	Enabling Environments: what adults could provide
30-50 months	• Understands use of objects (e.g. *"What do we use to cut things?"*) • Shows understanding of prepositions such as 'under', 'on top', 'behind' by carrying out an action or selecting correct picture. • Responds to simple instructions, e.g. to get or put away an object. • Beginning to understand 'why' and 'how' questions.	• Prompt children's thinking and discussion through involvement in their play. • Talk to children about what they have been doing and help them to reflect upon and explain events, e.g. *"You told me this model was going to be a tractor. What's this lever for?"* • Give children clear directions and help them to deal with those involving more than one action, e.g. *"Put the cars away, please, then come and wash your hands and get ready for lunch"*. • When introducing a new activity, use mime and gesture to support language development. • Showing children a photograph of an activity such as hand washing helps to reinforce understanding. • Be aware that some children may watch another child in order to know what to do, rather than understanding it themselves.	• Set up shared experiences that children can reflect upon, e.g. visits, cooking, or stories that can be re-enacted. • Help children to predict and order events coherently, by providing props and materials that encourage children to re-enact, using talk and action. • Find out from parents how children make themselves understood at home; confirm which their preferred language is. • Provide practical experiences that encourage children to ask and respond to questions, e.g. explaining pulleys or wet and dry sand. • Introduce, alongside books, story props, such as pictures, puppets and objects, to encourage children to retell stories and to think about how the characters feel.

40-60+ months	• Responds to instructions involving a two-part sequence. Understands humour, e.g. nonsense rhymes, jokes.
	• Able to follow a story without pictures or props.
	• Listens and responds to ideas expressed by others in conversation or discussion.
	
	Early Learning Goal
	Children follow instructions involving several ideas or actions. They answer 'how' and 'why' questions about their experiences and in response to stories or events.
		• Ask children to think in advance about how they will accomplish a task. Talk through and sequence the stages together.
		• Use stories from books to focus children's attention on predictions and explanations, e.g. *"Why did the boat tip over?"*
		• Help children to
		  ♦ identify patterns, e.g. what generally happens to 'good' and 'wicked' characters at the end of stories
		  ♦ draw conclusions: *"The sky has gone dark. It must be going to rain'*
		  ♦ explain effect: *'It sank because it was too heavy'*
		  ♦ predict: *'It might not grow in there if it is too dark'*
		  ♦ speculate: *'What if the bridge falls down?'*
			• Set up displays that remind children of what they have experienced, using objects, artefacts, photographs and books.
			• Provide for, initiate and join in imaginative play and role-play, encouraging children to talk about what is happening and to act out the scenarios in character.

Children develop at their own rates, and in their own ways. The development statements and their order should not be taken as necessary steps for individual children. They should not be used as checklists. The age/stage bands overlap because these are not fixed age boundaries but suggest a typical range of development.

Playing and Exploring, Active Learning, and Creating and Thinking Critically support children's learning across all areas

Communication and Language: Speaking

	A Unique Child: observing what a child is learning	Positive Relationships: what adults could do	Enabling Environments: what adults could provide
Birth - 11 months	• Communicates needs and feelings in a variety of ways including crying, gurgling, babbling and squealing. • Makes own sounds in response when talked to by familiar adults. • Lifts arms in anticipation of being picked up. • Practises and gradually develops speech sounds (babbling) to communicate with adults; says sounds like 'baba, nono, gogo'.	• Find out from parents how they like to communicate with their baby, noting especially the chosen language. • Ensure parents understand the importance of talking with babies in their home language. • Encourage babies' sounds and babbling by copying their sounds in a turn-taking 'conversation'. • Communicate with parents to exchange and update information about babies' personal words.	• Learn and use key words in the home languages of babies in the setting. • Provide tapes and tape recorders so that parents can record familiar, comforting sounds, such as lullabies in home languages. Use these to help babies settle if they are tired or distressed.
8-20 months	• Uses sounds in play, e.g. 'brrrm' for toy car. • Uses single words. • Frequently imitates words and sounds. • Enjoys babbling and increasingly experiments with using sounds and words to communicate for a range of purposes (e.g. teddy, more, no, bye-bye.) • Uses pointing with eye gaze to make requests, and to share an interest. • Creates personal words as they begin to develop language.	• Try to 'tune in' to the different messages young babies are attempting to convey. • Share the fun of discovery and value babies' attempts at words, e.g., by picking up a doll in response to "baba". • When babies try to say a word, repeat it back so they can hear the name of the object clearly. • Find out from parents greetings used in English and in languages other than English, and use them in the setting. • Recognise and equally value all languages spoken and written by parents, staff and children.	• Find out from parents the words that children use for things which are important to them, such as 'bankie' for their comfort blanket, remembering to extend this question to home languages. • Explain that strong foundations in a home language support the development of English.
16-26 months	• Copies familiar expressions, e.g. 'Oh dear', 'All gone'. • Beginning to put two words together (e.g. 'want ball', 'more juice'). • Uses different types of everyday words (nouns, verbs and adjectives, e.g. banana, go, sleep, hot). • Beginning to ask simple questions. • Beginning to talk about people and things that are not present.	• Build vocabulary by giving choices, e.g. 'apple or satsuma?' • Model building sentences by repeating what the child says and adding another word, e.g. child says 'car', say 'mummy's car' or 'blue car'. • Show children how to pronounce or use words by responding and repeating what they say in the correct way, rather than saying they are wrong. • Accept and praise words and phrases in home languages, saying English alternatives and encouraging their use. • Encourage parents whose children are learning English as an additional language to continue to encourage use of the first language at home. • Support children in using a variety of communication strategies, including signing, where appropriate.	• Allow time to follow young children's lead and have fun together while developing vocabulary, e.g. saying 'We're **jumping up**', 'going **down**'. • Plan to talk through and comment on some activities to highlight specific vocabulary or language structures, e.g. "You've caught the ball. I've caught the ball. Nasima's caught the ball". • Provide stories with repetitive phrases and structures to read aloud to children to support specific vocabulary or language structures.

Children develop at their own rates, and in their own ways. The development statements and their order should not be taken as necessary steps for individual children. They should not be used as checklists. The age/stage bands overlap because these are not fixed age boundaries but suggest a typical range of development.

Playing and Exploring, Active Learning, and Creating and Thinking Critically support children's learning across all areas

Communication and Language: Speaking

	A Unique Child: observing what a child is learning	Positive Relationships: what adults could do	Enabling Environments: what adults could provide
22-36 months	• Uses language as a powerful means of widening contacts, sharing feelings, experiences and thoughts. • Holds a conversation, jumping from topic to topic. • Learns new words very rapidly and is able to use them in communicating. • Uses gestures, sometimes with limited talk, e.g. reaches toward toy, saying 'I have it'. • Uses a variety of questions (e.g. *what, where, who*). • Uses simple sentences (e.g.' *Mummy gonna work.*') • Beginning to use word endings (e.g. *going, cats*).	• Wait and allow the child time to start the conversation. • Follow the child's lead to talk about what they are interested in. • Give children 'thinking time'. Wait for them to think about what they want to say and put their thoughts into words, without jumping in too soon to say something yourself. • For children learning English as an additional language, value non-verbal communications and those offered in home languages. • Add words to what children say, e.g. child says '*Brush dolly hair*', you say '*Yes, Lucy is brushing dolly's hair.*'	• Display pictures and photographs showing familiar events, objects and activities and talk about them with the children. • Provide activities which help children to learn to distinguish differences in sounds, word patterns and rhythms. • Plan to encourage correct use of language by telling repetitive stories, and playing games which involve repetition of words or phrases. • Provide opportunities for children whose home language is other than English, to use that language. • Help children to build their vocabulary by extending the range of their experiences. • Ensure that all practitioners use correct grammar. • Foster children's enjoyment of spoken and written language by providing interesting and stimulating play opportunities.
30-50 months	• Beginning to use more complex sentences to link thoughts (e.g. *using and, because*). • Can retell a simple past event in correct order (e.g. *went down slide, hurt finger*). • Uses talk to connect ideas, explain what is happening and anticipate what might happen next, recall and relive past experiences. • Questions why things happen and gives explanations. Asks e.g. *who, what, when, how.* • Uses a range of tenses (e.g. *play, playing, will play, played*). • Uses intonation, rhythm and phrasing to make the meaning clear to others. • Uses vocabulary focused on objects and people that are of particular importance to them. • Builds up vocabulary that reflects the breadth of their experiences. • Uses talk in pretending that objects stand for something else in play, e.g, '*This box is my castle.*'	• Talk with children to make links between their body language and words, e.g. "*Your face does look cross. Has something upset you?*" • Introduce new words in the context of play and activities. • Use a lot of statements and fewer questions. When you do ask a question, use an open question with many possible answers. • Show interest in the words children use to communicate and describe their experiences. • Help children expand on what they say, introducing and reinforcing the use of more complex sentences.	

Children develop at their own rates, and in their own ways. The development statements and their order should not be taken as necessary steps for individual children. They should not be used as checklists. The age/stage bands overlap because these are not fixed age boundaries but suggest a typical range of development.

Playing and Exploring, Active Learning, and Creating and Thinking Critically support children's learning across all areas

Communication and Language: Speaking

	A Unique Child: observing what a child is learning	Positive Relationships: what adults could do	Enabling Environments: what adults could provide
40-60+ months	• Extends vocabulary, especially by grouping and naming, exploring the meaning and sounds of new words. • Uses language to imagine and recreate roles and experiences in play situations. • Links statements and sticks to a main theme or intention. • Uses talk to organise, sequence and clarify thinking, ideas, feelings and events. • Introduces a storyline or narrative into their play. **Early Learning Goal** **Children express themselves effectively, showing awareness of listeners' needs. They use past, present and future forms accurately when talking about events that have happened or are to happen in the future. They develop their own narratives and explanations by connecting ideas or events.**	• Support children's growing ability to express a wide range of feelings orally, and talk about their own experiences. • Encourage conversation with others and demonstrate appropriate conventions: turn-taking, waiting until someone else has finished, listening to others and using expressions such as *"please", "thank you"* and *"can I...?"*. At the same time, respond sensitively to social conventions used at home. • Show children how to use language for negotiating, by saying *"May I...?", "Would it be all right...?", "I think that..."* and *"Will you...?"* in your interactions with them. • Model language appropriates for different audiences, for example, a visitor. • Encourage children to predict possible endings to stories and events. • Encourage children to experiment with words and sounds, e.g. in nonsense rhymes. • Encourage children to develop narratives in their play, using words such as: *first, last, next, before, after, all, most, some, each, every.* • Encourage language play, e.g. through stories such as 'Goldilocks and the Three Bears' and action songs that require intonation. • Value children's contributions and use them to inform and shape the direction of discussions.	• Give time for children to initiate discussions from shared experiences and have conversations with each other. • Give thinking time for children to decide what they want to say and how they will say it. • Set up collaborative tasks, for example, construction, food activities or story-making through role-play. • Help children to talk about and plan how they will begin, what parts each will play and what materials they will need. • Decide on the key vocabulary linked to activities, and ensure that all staff regularly model its use in a range of contexts. • Provide opportunities for talking for a wide range of purposes, e.g. to present ideas to others as descriptions, explanations, instructions or justifications, and to discuss and plan individual or shared activities. • Provide opportunities for children to participate in meaningful speaking and listening activities. For example, children can take models that they have made to show children in another group or class and explain how they were made.

Children develop at their own rates, and in their own ways. The development statements and their order should not be taken as necessary steps for individual children. They should not be used as checklists. The age/stage bands overlap because these are not fixed age boundaries but suggest a typical range of development.

Playing and Exploring, Active Learning, and Creating and Thinking Critically support children's learning across all areas

Physical Development: Moving and Handling

	A Unique Child: observing what a child is learning	Positive Relationships: what adults could do	Enabling Environments: what adults could provide
Birth - 11 months	• Turns head in response to sounds and sights. • Gradually develops ability to hold up own head. • Makes movements with arms and legs which gradually become more controlled. • Rolls over from front to back, from back to front. • When lying on tummy becomes able to lift first head and then chest, supporting self with forearms and then straight arms. • Watches and explores hands and feet, e.g. when lying on back lifts legs into vertical position and grasps feet. • Reaches out for, touches and begins to hold objects. • Explores objects with mouth, often picking up an object and holding it to the mouth.	• Help babies to become aware of their own bodies through touch and movement, e.g. clapping the baby's hands together, gently shaking baby's foot. • Play games, such as offering a small toy and taking it again to rattle, or sail through the air. • Encourage young babies in their efforts to gradually share control of the bottle with you.	• Encourage babies to explore the space near them by putting interesting things beside them, such as crinkly paper, or light, soft material. • Let babies kick and stretch freely on their tummies and backs. • Have well-planned areas that allow babies maximum space to move, roll, stretch and explore in safety indoors and outdoors. • Provide resources that move or make a noise when touched to stimulate babies to reach out with their arms and legs. • Provide objects to be sucked, pulled, squeezed and held, to encourage the development of fine motor skills.
8-20 months	• Sits unsupported on the floor. • When sitting, can lean forward to pick up small toys. • Pulls to standing, holding on to furniture or person for support. • Crawls, bottom shuffles or rolls continuously to move around. • Walks around furniture lifting one foot and stepping sideways (cruising), and walks with one or both hands held by adult. • Takes first few steps independently. • Passes toys from one hand to the other. • Holds an object in each hand and brings them together in the middle, e.g. holds two blocks and bangs them together. • Picks up small objects between thumb and fingers. • Enjoys the sensory experience of making marks in damp sand, paste or paint. • Holds pen or crayon using a whole hand (palmar) grasp and makes random marks with different strokes.	• Engage babies in varied physical experiences, such as bouncing, rolling, rocking and splashing, both indoors and outdoors. • Encourage babies to use resources they can grasp, squeeze and throw. • Encourage babies to notice other babies and children coming and going near to them. • Support and encourage babies' drive to stand and walk. • Be aware that babies have little sense of danger when their interests are focused on getting something they want. • Use feeding, changing and bathing times to share finger plays, such as 'Round and Round the Garden'. • Show babies different ways to make marks in dough or paint by swirling, poking or patting it.	• Provide novelty in the environment that encourages babies to use all of their senses and move indoors and outdoors. • Offer low-level equipment so that babies can pull up to a standing position, shuffle or walk, ensuring that they are safe at all times, while not restricting their explorations. • Provide tunnels, slopes and low-level steps to stimulate and challenge toddlers. • Provide push-along toys and trundle trikes indoors and out. • Make toys easily accessible for children to reach and fetch. • Plan space to encourage free movement. • Provide resources that stimulate babies to handle and manipulate things, e.g. toys with buttons to press or books with flaps to open. • Use gloop (cornflour and water) in small trays so that babies can enjoy putting fingers into it and lifting them out.

Children develop at their own rates, and in their own ways. The development statements and their order should not be taken as necessary steps for individual children. They should not be used as checklists. The age/stage bands overlap because these are not fixed age boundaries but suggest a typical range of development.

Playing and Exploring, Active Learning, and Creating and Thinking Critically support children's learning across all areas

Physical Development: Moving and Handling

	A Unique Child: observing what a child is learning	Positive Relationships: what adults could do	Enabling Environments: what adults could provide
16-26 months	• Walks upstairs holding hand of adult. • Comes downstairs backwards on knees (crawling). • Beginning to balance blocks to build a small tower. • Makes connections between their movement and the marks they make.	• Encourage independence as young children explore particular patterns of movement, sometimes referred to as schemas. • Tell stories that encourage children to think about the way they move. • Treat mealtimes as an opportunity to help children to use fingers, spoon and cup to feed themselves. • Help young children to find comfortable ways of grasping, holding and using things they wish to use, such as a hammer, a paintbrush or a teapot in the home corner.	• Anticipate young children's exuberance and ensure the space is clear and suitable for their rapid and sometimes unpredictable movements. • Use music to stimulate exploration with rhythmic movements. • Provide different arrangements of toys and soft play materials to encourage crawling, tumbling, rolling and climbing. • Provide a range of wheeled toys indoors and outdoors, such as trundle trikes, buggies for dolls, push carts. • Provide items for filling, emptying and carrying, such as small paper carrier bags, baskets and buckets. • Provide materials that enable children to help with chores such as sweeping, pouring, digging or feeding pets. • Provide sticks, rollers and moulds for young children to use in dough, clay or sand.
22-36 months	• Runs safely on whole foot. • Squats with steadiness to rest or play with object on the ground, and rises to feet without using hands. • Climbs confidently and is beginning to pull themselves up on nursery play climbing equipment. • Can kick a large ball. • Turns pages in a book, sometimes several at once. • Shows control in holding and using jugs to pour, hammers, books and mark-making tools. • Beginning to use three fingers (tripod grip) to hold writing tools • Imitates drawing simple shapes such as circles and lines. • Walks upstairs or downstairs holding onto a rail two feet to a step. • May be beginning to show preference for dominant hand.	• Be aware that children can be very energetic for short bursts and need periods of rest and relaxation. • Value the ways children choose to move. • Give as much opportunity as possible for children to move freely between indoors and outdoors. • Talk to children about their movements and help them to explore new ways of moving, such as squirming, slithering and twisting along the ground like a snake, and moving quickly, slowly or on tiptoe. • Encourage body tension activities such as stretching, reaching, curling, twisting and turning. • Be alert to the safety of children, particularly those who might overstretch themselves. • Encourage children in their efforts to do up buttons, pour a drink, and manipulate objects in their play, e.g. '*Can you put the dolly's arm in the coat?*'	• Plan opportunities for children to tackle a range of levels and surfaces including flat and hilly ground, grass, pebbles, asphalt, smooth floors and carpets. • Provide a range of large play equipment that can be used in different ways, such as boxes, ladders, A-frames and barrels. • Plan time for children to experiment with equipment and to practise movements they choose. • Provide safe spaces and explain safety to children and parents. • Provide real and role-play opportunities for children to create pathways, e.g. road layouts, or going on a picnic. • Provide CD and tape players, scarves, streamers and musical instruments so that children can respond spontaneously to music. • Plan activities that involve moving and stopping, such as musical bumps. • Provide 'tool boxes' containing things that make marks, so that children can explore their use both indoors and outdoors.

Children develop at their own rates, and in their own ways. The development statements and their order should not be taken as necessary steps for individual children. They should not be used as checklists. The age/stage bands overlap because these are not fixed age boundaries but suggest a typical range of development.

Playing and Exploring, Active Learning, and Creating and Thinking Critically support children's learning across all areas

Physical Development: Moving and Handling

	A Unique Child: observing what a child is learning	Positive Relationships: what adults could do	Enabling Environments: what adults could provide
30-50 months	• Moves freely and with pleasure and confidence in a range of ways, such as slithering, shuffling, rolling, crawling, walking, running, jumping, skipping, sliding and hopping. • Mounts stairs, steps or climbing equipment using alternate feet. • Walks downstairs, two feet to each step while carrying a small object. • Runs skilfully and negotiates space successfully, adjusting speed or direction to avoid obstacles. • Can stand momentarily on one foot when shown. • Can catch a large ball. • Draws lines and circles using gross motor movements. • Uses one-handed tools and equipment, e.g. makes snips in paper with child scissors. • Holds pencil between thumb and two fingers, no longer using whole-hand grasp. • Holds pencil near point between first two fingers and thumb and uses it with good control. • Can copy some letters, e.g. letters from their name.	• Encourage children to move with controlled effort, and use associated vocabulary such as 'strong', 'firm', 'gentle', 'heavy', 'stretch', 'reach', 'tense and 'floppy'. • Use music of different styles and cultures to create moods and talk about how people move when they are sad, happy or cross. • Motivate children to be active through games such as follow the leader. • Talk about why children should take care when moving freely. • Teach children the skills they need to use equipment safely, e.g. cutting with scissors or using tools. • Encourage children to use the vocabulary of movement, e.g. 'gallop', 'slither', of instruction e.g. 'follow', 'lead' and 'copy'. w	• Provide time and space to enjoy energetic play daily. • Provide large portable equipment that children can move about safely and cooperatively to create their own structures, such as milk crates, tyres, large cardboard tubes. • Practise movement skills through games with beanbags, cones, balls and hoops. • Plan activities where children can practise moving in different ways and at different speeds, balancing, target throwing, rolling, kicking and catching • Provide sufficient equipment for children to share, so that waiting to take turns does not spoil enjoyment. • Mark out boundaries for some activities, such as games involving wheeled toys or balls, so that children can more easily regulate their own activities.
40-60+ months	• Experiments with different ways of moving. • Jumps off an object and lands appropriately. • Negotiates space successfully when playing racing and chasing games with other children, adjusting speed or changing direction to avoid obstacles. • Travels with confidence and skill around, under, over and through balancing and climbing equipment. • Shows increasing control over an object in pushing, patting, throwing, catching or kicking it. • Uses simple tools to effect changes to materials. • Handles tools, objects, construction and malleable materials safely and with increasing control. • Shows a preference for a dominant hand. • Begins to use anticlockwise movement and retrace vertical lines. • Begins to form recognisable letters. • Uses a pencil and holds it effectively to form recognisable letters, most of which are correctly formed.	• Pose challenging questions such as 'Can you get all the way round the climbing frame without your knees touching it?' • Talk with children about the need to match their actions to the space they are in. • Show children how to collaborate in throwing, rolling, fetching and receiving games, encouraging children to play with one another once their skills are sufficient. • Introduce and encourage children to use the vocabulary of manipulation, e.g. 'squeeze' and 'prod.' • Explain why safety is an important factor in handling tools, equipment and materials, and have sensible rules for everybody to follow.	• Provide activities that give children the opportunity and motivation to practise manipulative skills, e.g. cooking, painting, clay and playing instruments. • Provide play resources including small-world toys, construction sets, threading and posting toys, dolls' clothes and material for collage. • Teach children skills of how to use tools and materials effectively and safely and give them opportunities to practise them. • Provide a range of left-handed tools, especially left-handed scissors, as needed. • Support children with physical difficulties with nonslip mats, small trays for equipment, and triangular or thicker writing tools. • Provide a range of construction toys of different sizes, made of wood, rubber or plastic, that fix together in a variety of ways, e.g. by twisting, pushing, slotting or magnetism.

Early Learning Goal

Children show good control and co-ordination in large and small movements. They move confidently in a range of ways, safely negotiating space. They handle equipment and tools effectively, including pencils for writing.

Children develop at their own rates, and in their own ways. The development statements and their order should not be taken as necessary steps for individual children. They should not be used as checklists. The age/stage bands overlap because these are not fixed age boundaries but suggest a typical range of development.

Playing and Exploring, Active Learning, and Creating and Thinking Critically support children's learning across all areas

Physical Development: Health and self-care

		A Unique Child: observing what a child is learning	Positive Relationships: what adults could do	Enabling Environments: what adults could provide
Birth - 11 months		• Responds to and thrives on warm, sensitive physical contact and care. • Expresses discomfort, hunger or thirst. • Anticipates food routines with interest.	• Encourage babies gradually to share control of food and drink. • Talk to parents about the feeding patterns of young babies. • Talk to young babies as you stroke their cheeks, or pat their backs, reminding them that you are there and they are safe. • Notice individual baby cues when spending special one-to-one time with them to ensure they are ready to engage. • Discuss the cultural needs and expectations for skin and hair care with parents prior to entry to the setting, ensuring that the needs of all children are met appropriately and that parents' wishes are respected. • Be aware of specific health difficulties among the babies in the group.	• Plan to take account of the individual cultural and feeding needs of young babies in your group. • There may be considerable variation in the way parents feed their children at home. Remember that some parents may need interpreter support. • Trained staff can introduce baby massage sessions that make young babies feel nurtured and promote a sense of well-being. Involving parents helps them to use this approach at home.
8-20 months		• Opens mouth for spoon. • Holds own bottle or cup. • Grasps finger foods and brings them to mouth. • Attempts to use spoon: can guide towards mouth but food often falls off. • Can actively cooperate with nappy changing (lies still, helps hold legs up). • Starts to communicate urination, bowel movement.	• Talk to parents about how their baby communicates needs. Ensure that parents and carers who speak languages other than English are able to share their views. • Help children to enjoy their food and appreciate healthier choices by combining favourites with new tastes and textures.. • Be aware that babies have little sense of danger when their interests are focused on getting something they want.	• Provide a comfortable, accessible place where babies can rest or sleep when they want to. • Plan alternative activities for babies who do not need sleep at the same time as others do. • Ensure mealtime seating allows young children to have feet firmly on the floor or foot rest. This aids stability and upper trunk control supporting hand-to-mouth co-ordination. • Provide safe surroundings in which young children have freedom to move as they want, while being kept safe by watchful adults.
16-26 months		• Develops own likes and dislikes in food and drink. • Willing to try new food textures and tastes. • Holds cup with both hands and drinks without much spilling. • Clearly communicates wet or soiled nappy or pants. • Shows some awareness of bladder and bowel urges. • Shows awareness of what a potty or toilet is used for. • Shows a desire to help with dressing/undressing and hygiene routines.	• Encourage efforts such as when a young child offers their arm to put in a coat sleeve. • Be aware of and learn about differences in cultural attitudes to children's developing independence. • Discuss cultural expectations for toileting, since in some cultures young boys may be used to sitting rather than standing at the toilet. • Value children's choices and encourage them to try something new and healthy.	• Ensure that there is time for young children to complete a self-chosen task, such as trying to put on their own shoes. • Establish routines that enable children to look after themselves, e.g. putting their clothes and aprons on hooks or washing themselves. • Create time to discuss options so that young children have choices between healthy options, such as whether they will drink water or milk. • Place water containers where children can find them easily and get a drink when they need one.

Children develop at their own rates, and in their own ways. The development statements and their order should not be taken as necessary steps for individual children. They should not be used as checklists. The age/stage bands overlap because these are not fixed age boundaries but suggest a typical range of development.

Playing and Exploring, Active Learning, and Creating and Thinking Critically support children's learning across all areas

Physical Development: Health and self-care

	A Unique Child: observing what a child is learning	Positive Relationships: what adults could do	Enabling Environments: what adults could provide
22-36 months	• Feeds self competently with spoon. • Drinks well without spilling. • Clearly communicates their need for potty or toilet. • Beginning to recognise danger and seeks support of significant adults for help. • Helps with clothing, e.g. puts on hat, unzips zipper on jacket, takes off unbuttoned shirt. • Beginning to be independent in self-care, but still often needs adult support.	• Respond to how child communicates need for food, drinks, toileting and when uncomfortable. • Support parents' routines with young children's toileting by having flexible routines and by encouraging children's efforts at independence. • Support children's growing independence as they do things for themselves, such as pulling up their pants after toileting, recognising differing parental expectations. • Involve young children in preparing food. • Give children the chance to talk about what they like to eat, while reinforcing messages about healthier choices. • Remember that children who have limited opportunity to play outdoors may lack a sense of danger.	• Allow children to pour their own drinks, serve their own food, choose a story, hold a puppet or water a plant. • Offer choices for children in terms of potties, trainer seats or steps. • Create opportunities for moving towards independence, e.g. have hand-washing facilities safely within reach. • Provide pictures or objects representing options to support children in making and expressing choices. • Choose some stories that highlight the consequences of choices. • Ensure children's safety, while not unduly inhibiting their risk-taking. • Display a colourful daily menu showing healthy meals and snacks and discuss choices with the children, reminding them, e.g. that they tried something previously and might like to try it again or encouraging them to try something new. • Be aware of eating habits at home and of the different ways people eat their food, e.g. that eating with clean fingers is as skilled and equally valued as using cutlery.
30-50 months	• Can tell adults when hungry or tired or when they want to rest or play. • Observes the effects of activity on their bodies. • Understands that equipment and tools have to be used safely. • Gains more bowel and bladder control and can attend to toileting needs most of the time themselves. • Can usually manage washing and drying hands. • Dresses with help, e.g. puts arms into open-fronted coat or shirt when held up, pulls up own trousers, and pulls up zipper once it is fastened at the bottom.	• Talk with children about why you encourage them to rest when they are tired or why they need to wear wellingtons when it is muddy outdoors. • Encourage children to notice the changes in their bodies after exercise, such as their heart beating faster. • Talk with children about the importance of hand-washing. • Help children who are struggling with self-care by leaving a last small step for them to complete, e.g. pulling up their trousers from just below the waist.	• Provide a cosy place with a cushion and a soft light where a child can rest quietly if they need to. • Plan so that children can be active in a range of ways, including while using a wheelchair. • Encourage children to be active and energetic by organising lively games, since physical activity is important in maintaining good health and in guarding against children becoming overweight or obese in later life.

Children develop at their own rates, and in their own ways. The development statements and their order should not be taken as necessary steps for individual children. They should not be used as checklists. The age/stage bands overlap because these are not fixed age boundaries but suggest a typical range of development.

Playing and Exploring, Active Learning, and Creating and Thinking Critically support children's learning across all areas

Physical Development: Health and self-care

A Unique Child: observing what a child is learning	Positive Relationships: what adults could do	Enabling Environments: what adults could provide
40-60+ months • Eats a healthy range of foodstuffs and understands need for variety in food. • Usually dry and clean during the day. • Shows some understanding that good practices with regard to exercise, eating, sleeping and hygiene can contribute to good health. • Shows understanding of the need for safety when tackling new challenges, and considers and manages some risks. • Shows understanding of how to transport and store equipment safely. • Practices some appropriate safety measures without direct supervision. **Early Learning Goal** **Children know the importance for good health of physical exercise, and a healthy diet, and talk about ways to keep healthy and safe. They manage their own basic hygiene and personal needs successfully, including dressing and going to the toilet independently.**	• Acknowledge and encourage children's efforts to manage their personal needs, and to use and return resources appropriately. • Promote health awareness by talking with children about exercise, its effect on their bodies and the positive contribution it can make to their health. • Be sensitive to varying family expectations and life patterns when encouraging thinking about health. • Discuss with children why they get hot and encourage them to think about the effects of the environment, such as whether opening a window helps everybody to be cooler.	• Plan opportunities, particularly after exercise, for children to talk about how their bodies feel. • Find ways to involve children so that they are all able to be active in ways that interest them and match their health and ability.

Children develop at their own rates, and in their own ways. The development statements and their order should not be taken as necessary steps for individual children. They should not be used as checklists. The age/stage bands overlap because these are not fixed age boundaries but suggest a typical range of development.

Playing and Exploring, Active Learning, and Creating and Thinking Critically support children's learning across all areas

Literacy: Reading

	A Unique Child: observing what a child is learning	Positive Relationships: what adults could do	Enabling Environments: what adults could provide
Birth - 11 months	• Enjoys looking at books and other printed material with familiar people.	• Use finger play, rhymes and familiar songs from home to support young babies' enjoyment.	• Collect a range of board books, cloth books and stories to share with young babies.
8-20 months	• Handles books and printed material with interest.	• Notice and support babies' developing responses as they learn to anticipate and join in with finger and word play.	• Let children handle books and draw their attention to pictures. • Tell, as well as read, stories, looking at and interacting with young babies. • Make family books using small photo albums with photos of family members, significant people in the child's life, familiar everyday objects.
16-26 months	• Interested in books and rhymes and may have favourites.	• Encourage and support children's responses to picture books and stories you read with them. • Use different voices to tell stories and encourage young children to join in wherever possible.	• Provide CDs of rhymes, stories, sounds and spoken words. • Provide picture books, books with flaps or hidden words, books with accompanying CDs and story sacks. • Provide story sacks for parents to take them home to encourage use of books and talk about stories.
22-36 months	• Has some favourite stories, rhymes, songs, poems or jingles. • Repeats words or phrases from familiar stories. • Fills in the missing word or phrase in a known rhyme, story or game, e.g. 'Humpty Dumpty sat on a ...'.	• Encourage children to use the stories they hear in their play. • Read stories that children already know, pausing at intervals to encourage them to 'read' the next word.	• Create an attractive book area where children and adults can enjoy books together. • Find opportunities to tell and read stories to children, using puppets, soft toys, or real objects as props. • Provide stories, pictures and puppets which allow children to experience and talk about how characters feel.

Children develop at their own rates, and in their own ways. The development statements and their order should not be taken as necessary steps for individual children. They should not be used as checklists. The age/stage bands overlap because these are not fixed age boundaries but suggest a typical range of development.

Playing and Exploring, Active Learning, and Creating and Thinking Critically support children's learning across all areas

Literacy: Reading

	A Unique Child: observing what a child is learning	Positive Relationships: what adults could do	Enabling Environments: what adults could provide
30-50 months	• Enjoys rhyming and rhythmic activities. • Shows awareness of rhyme and alliteration. • Recognises rhythm in spoken words. • Listens to and joins in with stories and poems, one-to-one and also in small groups. • Joins in with repeated refrains and anticipates key events and phrases in rhymes and stories. • Beginning to be aware of the way stories are structured. • Suggests how the story might end. • Listens to stories with increasing attention and recall. • Describes main story settings, events and principal characters. • Shows interest in illustrations and print in books and print in the environment. • Recognises familiar words and signs such as own name and advertising logos. • Looks at books independently. • Handles books carefully. • Knows information can be relayed in the form of print. • Holds books the correct way up and turns pages. • Knows that print carries meaning and, in English, is read from left to right and top to bottom.	• Focus on meaningful print such as a child's name, words on a cereal packet or a book title, in order to discuss similarities and differences between symbols. • Help children to understand what a word is by using names and labels and by pointing out words in the environment and in books. • Provide dual language books and read them with all children, to raise awareness of different scripts. Try to match dual language books to languages spoken by families in the setting. • Remember not all languages have written forms and not all families are literate either in English, or in a different home language. • Discuss with children the characters in books being read. • Encourage them to predict outcomes, to think of alternative endings and to compare plots and the feelings of characters with their own experiences. • Plan to include home language and bilingual story sessions by involving qualified bilingual adults, as well as enlisting the help of parents.	• Provide some simple poetry, song, fiction and non-fiction books. • Provide fact and fiction books in all areas, e.g. construction area as well as the book area. • Provide books containing photographs of the children that can be read by adults and that children can begin to 'read' by themselves. • Add child-made books and adult-scribed stories to the book area and use these for sharing stories with others. • Create an environment rich in print where children can learn about words, e.g. using names, signs, posters. • When children can see the text, e.g. using big books, model the language of print, such as *letter, word, page, beginning, end, first, last, middle*. • Introduce children to books and other materials that provide information or instructions. Carry out activities using instructions, such as reading a recipe to make a cake. • Ensure access to stories for all children by using a range of visual cues and story props.
40-60+ months	• Continues a rhyming string. • Hears and says the initial sound in words. • Can segment the sounds in simple words and blend them together and knows which letters represent some of them. • Links sounds to letters, naming and sounding the letters of the alphabet. • Begins to read words and simple sentences. • Uses vocabulary and forms of speech that are increasingly influenced by their experiences of books. • Enjoys an increasing range of books. • Knows that information can be retrieved from books and computers. **Early Learning Goal** **Children read and understand simple sentences. They use phonic knowledge to decode regular words and read them aloud accurately. They also read some common irregular words. They demonstrate understanding when talking with others about what they have read.**	• Discuss and model ways of finding out information from non-fiction texts. • Provide story sacks and boxes and make them with the children for use in the setting and at home. • Encourage children to recall words they see frequently, such as their own and friends' names. • Model oral blending of sounds to make words in everyday contexts, e.g. *'Can you get your h-a-t that?'* • Play games like word letter bingo to develop children's phoneme-grapheme correspondence. • Model to children how simple words can be segmented into sounds and blended together to make words. • Support and scaffold individual children's reading as opportunities arise.	• Encourage children to add to their first-hand experience of the world through the use of books, other texts and information, and information and communication technology (ICT). • Help children to identify the main events in a story and to enact stories, as the basis for further imaginative play. • Provide story boards and props which support children to talk about a story's characters and sequence of events. • When children are ready (usually, but not always, by the age of five) provide regular systematic synthetic phonics sessions. These should be multisensory in order to capture their interests, sustain motivation and reinforce learning. • Demonstrate using phonics as the prime approach to decode words while children can see the text, e.g. using big books. • Provide varied texts and encourage children to use all their skills including their phonic knowledge to decode words. • Provide some simple texts which children can decode to give them confidence and to practise their developing skills.

Children develop at their own rates, and in their own ways. The development statements and their order should not be taken as necessary steps for individual children. They should not be used as checklists. The age/stage bands overlap because these are not fixed age boundaries but suggest a typical range of development.

Playing and Exploring, Active Learning, and Creating and Thinking Critically support children's learning across all areas

Literacy: Writing

	A Unique Child: observing what a child is learning	Positive Relationships: what adults could do	Enabling Environments: what adults could provide
Birth - 11 months	*Children's later writing is based on skills and understandings which they develop as babies and toddlers. Before they can write, they need to learn to use spoken language to communicate. Later they learn to write down the words they can say. (See the roots of Writing in Communication and language).*	See Communication and Language	See Communication and Language
8-20 months	*Early mark-making is not the same as writing.It is a sensory and physical experience for babies and toddlers, which they do not yet connect to forming symbols which can communicate meaning. (See roots of mark-making and handwriting in Playing and exploring and Physical Development).*		
16-26 months	• Distinguishes between the different marks they make.	• Listen and support what children tell you about the marks they make.	
22-36 months			• Draw attention to marks, signs and symbols in the environment and talk about what they represent. Ensure this involves recognition of English and other relevant scripts. • Provide materials which reflect a cultural spread, so that children see symbols and marks with which they are familiar, e.g. Chinese script on a shopping bag.

Children develop at their own rates, and in their own ways. The development statements and their order should not be taken as necessary steps for individual children. They should not be used as checklists. The age/stage bands overlap because these are not fixed age boundaries but suggest a typical range of development

Playing and Exploring, Active Learning, and Creating and Thinking Critically support children's learning across all areas

Literacy: Writing

	A Unique Child: observing what a child is learning	Positive Relationships: what adults could do	Enabling Environments: what adults could provide
30-50 months	• Sometimes gives meaning to marks as they draw and paint. • Ascribes meanings to marks that they see in different places.	• Notice and encourage the marks children make and the meanings that they give to them, such as when a child covers a whole piece of paper and says, "I'm writing". • Support children in recognising and writing their own names. • Make books with children of activities they have been doing, using photographs of them as illustrations.	• Write down things children say to support their developing understanding that what they say can be written down and then read and understood by someone else. Encourage parents to do this as well. • Model writing for a purpose, e.g. a shopping list, message for parents, or reminder for ourselves. • Model writing poems and short stories, writing down ideas suggested by the children. • Provide activities during which children will experiment with writing, for example, leaving a message. • Include opportunities for writing during role-play and other activities. • Encourage the children to use their phonic knowledge when writing.
40-60+ months	• Gives meaning to marks they make as they draw, write and paint. • Begins to break the flow of speech into words. • Continues a rhyming string. • Hears and says the initial sound in words. • Can segment the sounds in simple words and blend them together. • Links sounds to letters, naming and sounding the letters of the alphabet. • Uses some clearly identifiable letters to communicate meaning, representing some sounds correctly and in sequence. • Writes own name and other things such as labels, captions. • Attempts to write short sentences in meaningful contexts. **Early Learning Goal** **Children use their phonic knowledge to write words in ways which match their spoken sounds. They also write some irregular common words. They write simple sentences which can be read by themselves and others. Some words are spelt correctly and others are phonetically plausible.**	• Talk to children about the letters that represent the sounds they hear at the beginning of their own names and other familiar words. • Demonstrate writing so that children can see spelling in action. • Demonstrate how to segment the sounds(phonemes) in simple words and how the sounds are represented by letters (graphemes). • Expect them to apply their own grapheme/phoneme knowledge to what they write in meaningful contexts. • Support and scaffold individual children's writing as opportunities arise.	• Provide word banks and writing resources for both indoor and outdoor play. • Provide a range of opportunities to write for different purposes about things that interest children. • Resource role-play areas with listening and writing equipment Ensure that role-play areas encourage writing of signs with a real purpose, e.g. a pet shop. • Plan fun activities and games that help children create rhyming strings of real and imaginary words, e.g. *Maddie, daddy, baddie, laddie.* • When children are ready (usually, but not always, by the age of five) provide regular systematic synthetic phonics sessions. These should be multisensory in order to capture their interests, sustain motivation and reinforce learning.

Children develop at their own rates, and in their own ways. The development statements and their order should not be taken as necessary steps for individual children. They should not be used as checklists. The age/stage bands overlap because these are not fixed age boundaries but suggest a typical range of development.

Playing and Exploring, Active Learning, and Creating and Thinking Critically support children's learning across all areas

Mathematics: Numbers

	A Unique Child: observing what a child is learning	Positive Relationships: what adults could do	Enabling Environments: what adults could provide
Birth - 11 months	• Notices changes in number of objects/images or sounds in group of up to 3.	• Sing number rhymes as you dress or change babies, e.g. 'One, Two, Buckle My Shoe'. • Move with babies to the rhythm patterns in familiar songs and rhymes. • Encourage babies to join in tapping and clapping along to simple rhythms.	• Display favourite things so that a young baby can see them. • Provide a small group of the same objects in treasure baskets, as well as single items, e.g. two fir cones or three shells. • Create a mobile, occasionally changing the number of items you hang on it. • Collect number rhymes which are repetitive and are related to children's actions and experiences, for example, 'Peter Hammers with One Hammer'. • Use song and rhymes during personal routines, e.g. 'Two Little Eyes to Look Around', pointing to their eyes, one by one. • Collect number and counting rhymes from a range of cultures and in other languages. This will benefit all children and will give additional support for children learning English as an additional language.
8-20 months	• Develops an awareness of number names through their enjoyment of action rhymes and songs that relate to their experience of numbers. • Has some understanding that things exist, even when out of sight.		
16-26 months	• Knows that things exist, even when out of sight. • Beginning to organise and categorise objects, e.g. putting all the teddy bears together or teddies and cars in separate piles. • Says some counting words randomly.	• Use number words in meaningful contexts, e.g. 'Here is your other mitten. Now we have two'. • Talk to young children about 'lots' and 'few' as they play. • Talk about young children's choices and, where appropriate, demonstrate how counting helps us to find out how many. • Talk about the maths in everyday situations, e.g. doing up a coat, one hole for each button. • Tell parents about all the ways children learn about numbers in your setting. Have interpreter support or translated materials to support children and families learning English as an additional language	• Provide varied opportunities to explore 'lots' and 'few' in play. • Equip the role-play area with things that can be sorted in different ways. • Provide collections of objects that can be sorted and matched in various ways. • Provide resources that support children in making one-to-one correspondences, e.g. giving each dolly a cup.
22-36 months	• Selects a small number of objects from a group when asked, for example, please give me one', 'please give me two'. • Recites some number names in sequence. • Creates and experiments with symbols and marks representing ideas of number. • Begins to make comparisons between quantities. • Uses some language of quantities, such as 'more' and 'a lot'. • Knows that a group of things changes in quantity when something is added or taken away.	• Encourage parents of children learning English as an additional language to talk in their home language about quantities and numbers. • Sing counting songs and rhymes which help to develop children's understanding of number, such as 'Two Little Dickie Birds'. • Play games which relate to number order, addition and subtraction, such as hopscotch and skittles and target games.	• Make a display with the children about their favourite things. Talk about how many like apples, or which of them watches a particular TV programme at home. • Provide props for children to act out counting songs and rhymes. • Provide games and equipment that offer opportunities for counting, such as skittles. • Plan to incorporate a mathematical component in areas such as the sand, water or other play areas.

Children develop at their own rates, and in their own ways. The development statements and their order should not be taken as necessary steps for individual children. They should not be used as checklists. The age/stage bands overlap because these are not fixed are boundaries but suggest a typical range of development

Playing and Exploring, Active Learning, and Creating and Thinking Critically support children's learning across all areas

Mathematics: Numbers

	A Unique Child: observing what a child is learning	Positive Relationships: what adults could do	Enabling Environments: what adults could provide
30-50 months	• Uses some number names and number language spontaneously. • Uses some number names accurately in play. • Recites numbers in order to 10. • Knows that numbers identify how many objects are in a set. • Beginning to represent numbers using fingers, marks on paper or pictures. • Sometimes matches numeral and quantity correctly. • Shows curiosity about numbers by offering comments or asking questions. • Compares two groups of objects, saying when they have the same number. • Shows an interest in number problems. • Separates a group of three or four objects in different ways, beginning to recognise that the total is still the same. • Shows an interest in numerals in the environment. • Shows an interest in representing numbers. • Realises not only objects, but anything can be counted, including steps, claps or jumps.	• Use number language, e.g. 'one', 'two', 'three', 'lots', 'fewer', 'hundreds', 'how many?' and 'count' in a variety of situations. • Support children's developing understanding of abstraction by counting things that are not objects, such as hops, jumps, clicks or claps. • Model counting of objects in a random layout, showing the result is always the same as long as each object is only counted once. • Model and encourage use of mathematical language e.g. asking questions such as 'How many saucepans will fit on the shelf?' • Help children to understand that one thing can be shared by number of pieces, e.g. a pizza. • As you read number stories or rhymes, ask e.g. "When one more frog jumps in, how many will there be in the pool altogether?" • Use pictures and objects to illustrate counting songs, rhymes and number stories. • Encourage children to use mark-making to support their thinking about numbers and simple problems. • Talk with children about the strategies they are using, e.g. to work out a solution to a simple problem by using fingers or counting aloud.	• Give children a reason to count, e.g. by asking them to select enough wrist bands for three friends to play with the puppets. • Enable children to note the 'missing set', e.g. 'There are none left' when sharing things out. • Provide number labels for children to use, e.g. by putting a number label on each bike and a corresponding number on each parking space. • Include counting money and change in role-play games. • Create opportunities for children to separate objects into unequal groups as well as equal groups. • Provide story props that children can use in their play, e.g. varieties of fruit and several baskets like Handa's in the story *Handa's Surprise* by Eileen Browne.
40-60+ months	• Recognise some numerals of personal significance. • Recognises numerals 1 to 5. • Counts up to three or four objects by saying one number name for each item. • Counts actions or objects which cannot be moved. • Counts objects to 10, and beginning to count beyond 10. • Counts out up to six objects from a larger group.	• Encourage estimation, e.g. estimate how many sandwiches to make for the picnic. • Encourage use of mathematical language, e.g. number names to ten: 'Have you got enough to give me three?' • Ensure that children are involved in making displays, e.g. making their own pictograms of lunch choices. Develop this as a 3D representation using bricks and discuss the most popular choices. • Add numerals to all areas of learning and development, e.g. to a display of a favourite story, such as 'The Three Billy Goats Gruff'.	• Provide collections of interesting things for children to sort, order, count and label in their play. • Display numerals in purposeful contexts, e.g. a sign showing how many children can play on a number track. • Use tactile numeral cards made from sandpaper, velvet or string. • Create opportunities for children to experiment with a number of objects, the written numeral and the written number word. Develop this through matching activities with a range of numbers, numerals and a selection of objects.

Children develop at their own rates, and in their own ways. The development statements and their order should not be taken as necessary steps for individual children. They should not be used as checklists. The age/stage bands overlap because these are not fixed age boundaries but suggest a typical range of development.

Playing and Exploring, Active Learning, and Creating and Thinking Critically support children's learning across all areas

Mathematics: Numbers

A Unique Child: observing what a child is learning	Positive Relationships: what adults could do	Enabling Environments: what adults could provide
• Selects the correct numeral to represent 1 to 5, then 1 to 10 objects. • Counts an irregular arrangement of up to ten objects. • Estimates how many objects they can see and checks by counting them. • Uses the language of 'more' and 'fewer' to compare two sets of objects. • Finds the total number of items in two groups by counting all of them. • Says the number that is one more than a given number. • Finds one more or one less from a group of up to five objects, then ten objects. • In practical activities and discussion, beginning to use the vocabulary involved in adding and subtracting. • Records, using marks that they can interpret and explain. • Begins to identify own mathematical problems based on own interests and fascinations. **Early Learning Goal** **Children count reliably with numbers from one to 20, place them in order and say which number is one more or one less than a given number. Using quantities and objects, they add and subtract two single-digit numbers and count on or back to find the answer. They solve problems, including doubling, halving and sharing.**	• Make books about numbers that have meaning for the child such as favourite numbers, birth dates or telephone numbers. • Use rhymes, songs and stories involving counting on and counting back in ones, twos, fives and tens. • Emphasise the empty set and introduce the concept of nothing or zero. • Show interest in how children solve problems and value their different solutions. • Make sure children are secure about the order of numbers before asking what comes after or before each number. • Discuss with children how problems relate to others they have met, and their different solutions. • Talk about the methods children use to answer a problem they have posed, e.g. 'Get one more, and then we will both have two.' • Encourage children to make up their own story problems for other children to solve. • Encourage children to extend problems, e.g. "Suppose there were three people to share the bricks between instead of two". • Use mathematical vocabulary and demonstrate methods of recording, using standard notation where appropriate. • Give children learning English as additional language opportunities to work in their home language to ensure accurate understanding of concepts.	• Use a 100 square to show number patterns. • Encourage children to count the things they see and talk about and use numbers beyond ten • Make number games readily available and teach children how to use them. • Display interesting books about number. • Play games such as hide and seek that involve counting. • Encourage children to record what they have done, e.g. by drawing or tallying. • Use number staircases to show a starting point and how you arrive at another point when something is added or taken away. • Provide a wide range of number resources and encourage children to be creative in identifying and devising problems and solutions in all areas of learning. • Make number lines available for reference and encourage children to use them in their own play. • Big number lines may be more appropriate than counters for children with physical impairments. • Help children to understand that five fingers on each hand make a total of ten fingers altogether, or that two rows of three eggs in the box make six eggs altogether.

Children develop at their own rates, and in their own ways. The development statements and their order should not be taken as necessary steps for individual children. They should not be used as checklists. The age/stage bands overlap because these are not fixed age boundaries but suggest a typical range of development.

Playing and Exploring, Active Learning, and Creating and Thinking Critically support children's learning across all areas

Mathematics: Shape, space and measure

A Unique Child: observing what a child is learning	Positive Relationships: what adults could do	Enabling Environments: what adults could provide
Babies' early awareness of shape, space and measure grows from their sensory awareness and opportunities to observe objects and their movements, and to play and explore.		

Birth – 11 months

A Unique Child: observing what a child is learning	Positive Relationships: what adults could do	Enabling Environments: what adults could provide
See Characteristics of Effective Learning - Playing and Exploring, *and* Physical Development.	See Characteristics of Effective Learning - Playing and Exploring, *and* Physical Development.	See Characteristics of Effective Learning - Playing and Exploring, *and* Physical Development.

8-20 months

A Unique Child: observing what a child is learning	Positive Relationships: what adults could do	Enabling Environments: what adults could provide
• Recognises big things and small things in meaningful contexts. • Gets to know and enjoy daily routines, such as getting-up time, mealtimes, nappy time, and bedtime.	• Play games that involve curling and stretching, popping up and bobbing down. • Encourage babies' explorations of the characteristics of objects, e.g. by rolling a ball to them. • Talk about what objects are like and how objects, such as a sponge, can change their shape by being squeezed or stretched.	• Provide a range of objects of various textures and weights in treasure baskets to excite and encourage babies' interests. • Look at books showing objects such as a big truck and a little truck; or a big cat and a small kitten. • Use story props to support all children and particularly those learning English as an additional language.

16-26 months

A Unique Child: observing what a child is learning	Positive Relationships: what adults could do	Enabling Environments: what adults could provide
• Attempts, sometimes successfully, to fit shapes into spaces on inset boards or jigsaw puzzles. • Uses blocks to create their own simple structures and arrangements. • Enjoys filling and emptying containers. • Associates a sequence of actions with daily routines. • Beginning to understand that things might happen 'now'.	• Use 'tidy up time' to promote logic and reasoning about where things fit in or are kept. • Talk to children, as they play with water or sand, to encourage them to think about when something is full, empty or holds more. • Help young children to create different arrangements in the layout of road and rail tracks. • Highlight patterns in daily activities and routines. • Help children use their bodies to explore shape, through touching, seeing and feeling shape in art, music and dance.	• Encourage children, when helping with domestic tasks, to put all the pieces of apple on one dish and all the pieces of celery on another for snacks. • Use pictures or shapes of objects to indicate where things are kept and encourage children to work out where things belong. • Provide different sizes and shapes of containers in water play, so that children can experiment with quantities and measures. • Offer a range of puzzles with large pieces and knobs or handles to support success in fitting shapes into spaces.

22-36 months

A Unique Child: observing what a child is learning	Positive Relationships: what adults could do	Enabling Environments: what adults could provide
• Notices simple shapes and patterns in pictures. • Beginning to categorise objects according to properties such as shape or size. • Begins to use the language of size. • Understands some talk about immediate past and future, e.g. 'before', 'later' or 'soon'. • Anticipates specific time-based events such as mealtimes or home time.	• Talk about and help children to recognise patterns. • Draw children's attention to the patterns e.g. square/oblong/square which emerges as you fold or unfold a tablecloth or napkin. • Use descriptive words like *'big'* and *'little'* in everyday play situations and through books and stories. • Be consistent in your use of vocabulary for weight and mass.	• Collect pictures that illustrate the use of shapes and patterns from a variety of cultures, e.g. Arabic designs. • Provide opportunities for children to measure time (sand timer), weight (balances) and length (standard and non-standard units). • Vary the volume and capacity equipment in the sand, water and other play areas to maintain interest. • Use coins for sorting on play trays and into bags, purses and containers.

Children develop at their own rates, and in their own ways. The development statements and their order should not be taken as necessary steps for individual children. They should not be used as checklists. The age/stage bands overlap because these are not fixed age boundaries but suggest a typical range of development.

Playing and Exploring, Active Learning, and Creating and Thinking Critically support children's learning across all areas

Mathematics: Shape, space and measure

	A Unique Child: observing what a child is learning	Positive Relationships: what adults could do	Enabling Environments: what adults could provide
			• Measure for a purpose, such as finding out whether a teddy will fit in a bed.
30-50 months	• Shows an interest in shape and space by playing with shapes or making arrangements with objects. • Shows awareness of similarities of shapes in the environment. • Uses positional language. • Shows interest in shape by sustained construction activity or by talking about shapes or arrangements. • Shows interest in shapes in the environment. • Uses shapes appropriately for tasks. • Beginning to talk about the shapes of everyday objects, e.g. 'round' and 'tall'.	• Demonstrate the language for shape, position and measures in discussions, e.g. 'sphere', 'shape', 'box', 'in', 'on', 'inside', 'under', long, longest', 'short', 'shorter', 'shortest', 'heavy', 'light', 'full' and 'empty'. • Find out and use equivalent terms for these in home languages. • Encourage children to talk about the shapes they see and use and how they are arranged and used in constructions. • Value children's constructions, e.g. helping to display them or taking photographs of them.	• Organise the environment to foster shape matching, e.g. pictures of different bricks on containers to show where they are kept. • Have large and small blocks and boxes available for construction both indoors and outdoors. • Play games involving children positioning themselves inside, behind, on top and so on. • Provide rich and varied opportunities for comparing length, weight, capacity and time. • Use stories such as Rosie's Walk by Pat Hutchins to talk about distance and stimulate discussion about non-standard units and the need for standard units. • Show pictures that have symmetry or pattern and talk to children about them.
40-60+ months	• Beginning to use mathematical names for 'solid' 3D shapes and 'flat' 2D shapes, and mathematical terms to describe shapes. • Selects a particular named shape. • Can describe their relative position such as 'behind' or 'next to'. • Orders two or three items by length or height. • Orders two items by weight or capacity. • Uses familiar objects and common shapes to create and recreate patterns and build models. • Uses everyday language related to time. • Beginning to use everyday language related to money. • Orders and sequences familiar events. • Measures short periods of time in simple ways. **Early Learning Goal** **Children use everyday language to talk about size, weight, capacity, position, distance, time and money to compare quantities and objects and to solve problems. They recognise, create and describe patterns. They explore characteristics of everyday objects and shapes and use mathematical language to describe them.**	• Ask 'silly' questions, e.g. show a tiny box and ask if there is a bicycle in it. • Play peek-a-boo, revealing shapes a little at a time and at different angles, asking children to say what they think the shape is, what else it could be or what it could not be. • Be a robot and ask children to give you instructions to get to somewhere. Let them have a turn at being the robot for you to instruct. • Introduce children to the use of mathematical names for 'solid' 3D shapes and 'flat' 2D shapes, and the mathematical terms to describe shapes. • Encourage children to use everyday words to describe position, e.g. when following pathways or playing with outdoor apparatus.	• Make books about shape, time and measure: shapes found in the environment; long and short things; things of a specific length; and ones about patterns, or comparing things that are heavier or lighter. • Have areas where children can explore the properties of objects and where they can weigh and measure, such as a cookery station or a building area. • Plan opportunities for children to describe and compare shapes, measures and distance. • Provide materials and resources for children to observe and describe patterns in the indoor and outdoor environment and in daily routines. • Provide a range of natural materials for children to arrange, compare and order.

Children develop at their own rates, and in their own ways. The development statements and their order should not be taken as necessary steps for individual children. They should not be used as checklists. The age/stage bands overlap because these are not fixed are boundaries but suggest a typical range of development.

Playing and Exploring, Active Learning, and Creating and Thinking Critically support children's learning across all areas

Understanding the world: People and communities

	A Unique Child: observing what a child is learning	Positive Relationships: what adults could do	Enabling Environments: what adults could provide
Birth - 11 months	The beginnings of understanding of People and communities lie in early attachment and other relationships. See Personal, Social and Emotional Development and Communication and Language.	See Personal, Social and Emotional Development and Communication and Language.	See Personal, Social and Emotional Development and Communication and Language.
8-20 months	• Is curious about people and shows interest in stories about themselves and their family. • Enjoys pictures and stories about themselves, their families and other people.	• Help children to learn each other's names, e.g: through songs and rhymes. • Be positive about differences between people and support children's acceptance of difference. Be aware that negative attitudes towards difference are learned from examples the children witness. • Ensure that each child is recognised as a valuable contributor to the group. • Celebrate and value cultural, religious and community events and experiences	• Provide opportunities for babies to see people and things beyond the baby room, including the activities of older children. • Collect stories for, and make books about, children in the group, showing things they like to do. • Provide books and resources which represent children's diverse backgrounds and which avoid negative stereotypes. • Make photographic books about the children in the setting and encourage parents to contribute to these. • Provide positive images of all children including those with diverse physical characteristics, including disabilities.
16-26 months			
22-36 months	• Has a sense of own immediate family and relations. • In pretend play, imitates everyday actions and events from own family and cultural background, e.g. making and drinking tea. • Beginning to have their own friends. • Learns that they have similarities and differences that connect them to, and distinguish them from, others.	• Talk to children about their friends, their families, and why they are important.	• Share photographs of children's families, friends, pets or favourite people. • Support children's understanding of difference and of empathy by using props such as puppets and dolls to tell stories about diverse experiences, ensuring that negative stereotyping is avoided.

Children develop at their own rates, and in their own ways. The development statements and their order should not be taken as necessary steps for individual children. They should not be used as checklists. The age/stage bands overlap because these are not fixed age boundaries but suggest a typical range of development.

Playing and Exploring, Active Learning, and Creating and Thinking Critically support children's learning across all areas

Understanding the world: People and communities

	A Unique Child: observing what a child is learning	Positive Relationships: what adults could do	Enabling Environments: what adults could provide
30-50 months	• Shows interest in the lives of people who are familiar to them. • Remembers and talks about significant events in their own experience. • Recognises and describes special times or events for family or friends. • Shows interest in different occupations and ways of life. • Knows some of the things that make them unique, and can talk about some of the similarities and differences in relation to friends or family.	• Encourage children to talk about their own home and community life, and to find out about other children's experiences. • Ensure that children learning English as an additional language have opportunities to express themselves in their home language some of the time. • Encourage children to develop positive relationships with community members, such as fire fighters who visit the setting	• Plan extra time for helping children in transition, such as when they move from one setting to another or between different groups in the same setting. • Provide activities and opportunities for children to share experiences and knowledge from different parts of their lives with each other. • Provide ways of preserving memories of special events, e.g. making a book, collecting photographs, tape recording, drawing and writing. • Invite children and families with experiences of living in other countries to bring in photographs and objects from their home cultures including those from family members living in different areas of the UK and abroad. • Ensure the use of modern photographs of parts of the world that are commonly stereotyped and misrepresented, • Help children to learn positive attitudes and challenge negative attitudes and stereotypes, e.g. using puppets, Persona Dolls, stories and books showing black heroes or disabled kings or queens or families with same sex parents, having a visit from a male midwife or female fire fighter.
40-60+ months	• Enjoys joining in with family customs and routines. **Early Learning Goal** **Children talk about past and present events in their own lives and in the lives of family members. They know that other children don't always enjoy the same things, and are sensitive to this. They know about similarities and differences between themselves and others, and among families, communities and traditions.**	• Encourage children to share their feelings and talk about why they respond to experiences in particular ways. • Explain carefully why some children may need extra help or support for some things, or why some children feel upset by a particular thing. • Help children and parents to see the ways in which their cultures and beliefs are similar, sharing and discussing practices, resources, celebrations and experiences. • Strengthen the positive impressions children have of their own cultures and faiths, and those of others in their community, by sharing and celebrating a range of practices and special events.	• Visit different parts of the local community, including areas where some children may be very knowledgeable, e.g. Chinese supermarket, local church, elders lunch club, Greek café. • Provide role-play areas with a variety of resources reflecting diversity. • Make a display with the children, showing all the people who make up the community of the setting. • Share stories that reflect the diversity of children's experiences. • Invite people from a range of cultural backgrounds to talk about aspects of their lives or the things they do in their work, such as a volunteer who helps people become familiar with the local area.

Children develop at their own rates, and in their own ways. The development statements and their order should not be taken as necessary steps for individual children. They should not be used as checklists. The age/stage bands overlap because these are not fixed because these are not fixed are boundaries but suggest a typical range of development

Playing and Exploring, Active Learning, and Creating and Thinking Critically support children's learning across all areas

Understanding the world: The world

	A Unique Child: observing what a child is learning	Positive Relationships: what adults could do	Enabling Environments: what adults could provide
Birth - 11 months	• Moves eyes, then head, to follow moving objects. • Reacts with abrupt change when a face or object suddenly disappears from view. • Looks around a room with interest; visually scans environment for novel, interesting objects and events. • Smiles with pleasure at recognisable playthings. • Repeats actions that have an effect, e.g. kicking or hitting a mobile or shaking a rattle. See also Characteristics of Effective Learning – Playing and Exploring, and Physical Development	• Encourage young babies' movements through your interactions, e.g. touching their fingers and toes and showing delight at their kicking and waving.	• Provide a range of everyday objects for babies to explore and investigate such as treasure baskets. • Provide novelty – make small changes in the predictable environment. • Provide spaces that give young babies different views of their surroundings, such as a soft play area, with different levels to explore.
8-20 months	• Closely observes what animals, people and vehicles do. • Watches toy being hidden and tries to find it. • Looks for dropped objects. • Becomes absorbed in combining objects, e.g. banging two objects or placing objects into containers. • Knows things are used in different ways, e.g. a ball for rolling or throwing, a toy car for pushing.	• Play hiding and finding games inside and outdoors. • Plan varied arrangements of equipment and materials that can be used with babies in a variety of ways to maintain interest and provide challenges. • Draw attention to things in different areas that stimulate interest, such as a patterned surface.	• Provide lift-the-flap books to show something hidden from view. • Provide a variety of interesting things for babies to see when they are looking around them, looking up at the ceiling or peering into a corner. • Display and talk about photographs of babies' favourite places.
16-26 months	• Explores objects by linking together different approaches: shaking, hitting, looking, feeling, tasting, mouthing, pulling, turning and poking. • Remembers where objects belong. • Matches parts of objects that fit together, e.g. puts lid on teapot.	• Talk with children about their responses to sights, sounds and smells in the environment and what they like about playing outdoors. • Encourage young children to explore puddles, trees and surfaces such as grass, concrete or pebbles.	• Develop the use of the outdoors so that young children can investigate features, e.g. a mound, a path or a wall. • Provide a collection of sets of items for children to explore how objects can be combined together in heuristic play sessions.
22-36 months	• Enjoys playing with small-world models such as a farm, a garage, or a train track. • Notices detailed features of objects in their environment.	• Tell stories about places and journeys.	• Make use of outdoor areas to give opportunities for investigations of the natural world, for example, provide chimes, streamers, windmills and bubbles to investigate the effects of wind. • Provide story and information books about places, such as a zoo or the beach, to remind children of visits to real places.

Children develop at their own rates, and in their own ways. The development statements and their order should not be taken as necessary steps for individual children. They should not be used as checklists. The age/stage bands overlap because these are not fixed age boundaries but suggest a typical range of development.

Playing and Exploring, Active Learning, and Creating and Thinking Critically support children's learning across all areas

Understanding the world: The world

		A Unique Child: observing what a child is learning	Positive Relationships: what adults could do	Enabling Environments: what adults could provide
30-50 months		• Comments and asks questions about aspects of their familiar world such as the place where they live or the natural world. • Can talk about some of the things they have observed such as plants, animals, natural and found objects. • Talks about why things happen and how things work. • Developing an understanding of growth, decay and changes over time. • Shows care and concern for living things and the environment.	• Use parents' knowledge to extend children's experiences of the world. • Support children with sensory impairment by providing supplementary experience and information to enhance their learning about the world around them. • Arouse awareness of features of the environment in the setting and immediate local area, e.g. make visits to shops or a park. • Introduce vocabulary to enable children to talk about their observations and to ask questions.	• Use the local area for exploring both the built and the natural environment. • Provide opportunities to observe things closely through a variety of means, including magnifiers and photographs. • Provide play maps and small world equipment for children to create their own environments. • Teach skills and knowledge in the context of practical activities, e.g. learning about the characteristics of liquids and solids by involving children in melting chocolate or cooking eggs.
40-60+ months		• Looks closely at similarities, differences, patterns and change. **Early Learning Goal** **Children know about similarities and differences in relation to places, objects, materials and living things. They talk about the features of their own immediate environment and how environments might vary from one another. They make observations of animals and plants and explain why some things occur, and talk about changes.**	• Help children to notice and discuss patterns around them, e.g. rubbings from grates, covers, or bricks. • Examine change over time, for example, growing plants, and change that may be reversed, e.g. melting ice. • Use appropriate words, e.g. *'town,' 'village', 'road', 'path', 'house', 'flat', 'temple' and 'synagogue',* to help children make distinctions in their observations. • Help children to find out about the environment by talking to people, examining photographs and simple maps and visiting local places. • Encourage children to express opinions on natural and built environments and give opportunities for them to hear different points of view on the quality of the environment. • Encourage the use of words that help children to express opinions, e.g. *'busy', 'quiet' and 'pollution'.* • Use correct terms so that, e.g. children will enjoy naming a chrysalis if the practitioner uses its correct name. • Pose carefully framed open-ended questions, such as *"How can we...?"* or *"What would happen if...?".*	• Give opportunities to record findings by, e.g. drawing, writing, making a model or photographing. • Provide stories that help children to make sense of different environments. • Provide stimuli and resources for children to create simple maps and plans, paintings, drawings and models of observations of known and imaginary landscapes. • Give opportunities to design practical, attractive environments, for example, taking care of the flowerbeds or organising equipment outdoors.

Children develop at their own rates, and in their own ways. The development statements and their order should not be taken as necessary steps for individual children. They should not be used as checklists. The age/stage bands overlap because these are not fixed age boundaries but suggest a typical range of development.

Playing and Exploring, Active Learning, and Creating and Thinking Critically support children's learning across all areas

Understanding the world: Technology

	A Unique Child: observing what a child is learning	Positive Relationships: what adults could do	Enabling Environments: what adults could provide
Birth - 11 months	*The beginnings of understanding technology lie in babies exploring and making sense of objects and how they behave.* See Characteristics of Effective Learning - Playing and Exploring and Creating and Thinking Critically	See Characteristics of Effective Learning - Playing and Exploring and Creating and Thinking Critically	See Characteristics of Effective Learning - Playing and Exploring and Creating and Thinking Critically
8-20 months	• Anticipates repeated sounds, sights and actions, e.g. when an adult demonstrates an action toy several times. • Shows interest in toys with buttons, flaps and simple mechanisms and beginning to learn to operate them.	• Comment on the ways in which young children investigate how to push, pull, lift or press parts of toys and domestic equipment. • Talk about the effect of children's actions, as they investigate what things can do.	• Have available robust resources with knobs, flaps, keys or shutters. • Incorporate technology resources that children recognise into their play, such as a camera.
16-26 months	• Seeks to acquire basic skills in turning on and operating some ICT equipment. • Operates mechanical toys, e.g. turns the knob on a wind-up toy or pulls back on a friction car.	• Support children in exploring the control technology of toys, e.g. toy electronic keyboard. • Talk about ICT apparatus, what it does, what they can do with it and how to use it safely.	• Provide safe equipment to play with, such as torches, transistor radios or karaoke machines. • Let children use machines like the photocopier to copy their own pictures.
22-36 months			

Children develop at their own rates, and in their own ways. The development statements and their order should not be taken as necessary steps for individual children. They should not be used as checklists. The age/stage bands overlap because these are not fixed age boundaries but suggest a typical range of development.

Playing and Exploring, Active Learning, and Creating and Thinking Critically support children's learning across all areas

Understanding the world: Technology

	A Unique Child: observing what a child is learning	Positive Relationships: what adults could do	Enabling Environments: what adults could provide
30-50 months	• Knows how to operate simple equipment, e.g. turns on CD player and uses remote control. • Shows an interest in technological toys with knobs or pulleys, or real objects such as cameras or mobile phones. • Shows skill in making toys work by pressing parts or lifting flaps to achieve effects such as sound, movements or new images. • Knows that information can be retrieved from computers	• Support and extend the skills children develop as they become familiar with simple equipment, such as twisting or turning a knob. • Draw young children's attention to pieces of ICT apparatus they see or that they use with adult supervision.	• When out in the locality, ask children to help to press the button at the pelican crossing, or speak into an intercom to tell somebody you have come back.
40-60+ months	• Completes a simple program on a computer. • Uses ICT hardware to interact with age-appropriate computer software. **Early Learning Goal** **Children recognise that a range of technology is used in places such as homes and schools. They select and use technology for particular purposes.**	• Encourage children to speculate on the reasons why things happen or how things work. • Support children to coordinate actions to use technology, for example, call a telephone number. • Teach and encourage children to click on different icons to cause things to happen in a computer program.	• Provide a range of materials and objects to play with that work in different ways for different purposes, for example, egg whisk, torch, other household implements, pulleys, construction kits and tape recorder. • Provide a range of programmable toys, as well as equipment involving ICT, such as computers.

Children develop at their own rates, and in their own ways. The development statements and their order should not be taken as necessary steps for individual children.
They should not be used as checklists. The age/stage bands overlap because these are not fixed are boundaries but suggest a typical span of development

Expressive arts and design: Exploring and using media and materials

	A Unique Child: observing what a child is learning	Positive Relationships: what adults could do	Enabling Environments: what adults could provide
	Babies explore media and materials as part of their exploration of the world around them. See Characteristics of Effective Learning – Playing and Exploring, Physical Development, Understanding the World – The World	See Characteristics of Effective Learning – Playing and Exploring, Physical Development, Understanding the World – The World	See Characteristics of Effective Learning – Playing and Exploring, Physical Development, Understanding the World – The World
Birth – 11 months	• Explores and experiments with a range of media through sensory exploration, and using whole body. • Move their whole bodies to sounds they enjoy, such as music or a regular beat. • Imitates and improvises actions they have observed, e.g. clapping or waving. • Begins to move to music, listen to or join in rhymes or songs. • Notices and is interested in the effects of making movements which leave marks.	• Encourage babies to join in tapping and clapping along to simple rhythms. • Notice the different ways babies move in response to sounds, e.g. patting the floor when on their tummy, flexing and relaxing their legs, or opening and closing their palms. • Encourage babies to make marks and to squeeze and feel media such as paint, gloop (cornflour and water), dough and bubbles.	• Have a range of puppets that can glide along the table, or dance around on the end of a fist in time to some lively music. • Place big sheets of plastic or paper on the floor so that babies can be near or crawl on to it to make marks. • Provide materials to encourage large motor movements, e.g. sprinkling, throwing or spreading paint, glue, torn paper or other materials.
8-20 months		• Listen with children to a variety of sounds, talking about favourite sounds, songs and music. • Introduce children to language to describe sounds and rhythm, e.g., loud and soft, fast and slow. • Accept wholeheartedly young children's creations and help them to see them as something unique and valuable • Make notes detailing the processes involved in a child's creations, to share with parents.	• Make a sound line using a variety of objects strung safely, that will make different sounds, such as wood, pans and plastic bottles filled with different things. • Provide a wide range of materials, resources and sensory experiences to enable children to explore colour, texture and space. • Provide space and time for movement and dance both indoors and outdoors.
16-26 months		• Help children to listen to music and watch dance when opportunities arise, encouraging them to focus on how sound and movement develop from feelings and ideas. • Encourage and support the inventive ways in which children add, or mix media, or wallow in a particular experience.	• Invite dancers and musicians from theatre groups, the locality or a nearby school so that children begin to experience live performances. • Draw on a wide range of musicians and story-tellers from a variety of cultural backgrounds to extend children's experiences and to reflect their cultural heritages.
22-36 months	• Joins in singing favourite songs. • Creates sounds by banging, shaking, tapping or blowing. • Shows an interest in the way musical instruments sound. • Experiments with blocks, colours and marks.		• Choose unusual or interesting materials and resources that inspire exploration such as textured wall coverings, raffia, string, translucent paper or water-based glues with colour added.

Children develop at their own rates, and in their own ways. The development statements and their order should not be taken as necessary steps for individual children. They should not be used as checklists. The age/stage bands overlap because these are not fixed age boundaries but suggest a typical range of development.

Playing and Exploring, Active Learning, and Creating and Thinking Critically support children's learning across all areas

Expressive arts and design: media and materials

Expressive arts and design: Exploring and using media and materials

	A Unique Child: observing what a child is learning	Positive Relationships: what adults could do	Enabling Environments: what adults could provide
30-50 months	• Enjoys joining in with dancing and ring games. • Sings a few familiar songs. • Beginning to move rhythmically. • Imitates movement in response to music. • Taps out simple repeated rhythms. • Explores and learns how sounds can be changed. • Explores colour and how colours can be changed. • Understands that they can use lines to enclose a space, and then begin to use these shapes to represent objects. • Beginning to be interested in and describe the texture of things. • Uses various construction materials. • Beginning to construct, stacking blocks vertically and horizontally, making enclosures and creating spaces. • Joins construction pieces together to build and balance. • Realises tools can be used for a purpose.	• Support children's responses to different textures, e.g. touching sections of a texture display with their fingers, or feeling it with their cheeks to get a sense of different properties. • Introduce vocabulary to enable children to talk about their observations and experiences, e.g. 'smooth' 'shiny' 'rough' 'prickly' 'flat' 'patterned' 'jagged', 'bumpy' 'soft' and 'hard'. • Talk about children's growing interest in and use of colour as they begin to find differences between colours. • Make suggestions and ask questions to extend children's ideas of what is possible, for example, "I wonder what would happen if... ". • Support children in thinking about what they want to make, the processes that may be involved and the materials and resources they might need, such as a photograph to remind them what the climbing frame is like.	• Lead imaginative movement sessions based on children's current interests such as space travel, zoo animals or shadows. • Provide a place where work in progress can be kept safely. • Talk with children about where they can see models and plans in the environment, such as at the local planning office, in the town square, or at the new apartments down the road. • Demonstrate and teach skills and techniques associated with the things children are doing, for example, show them how to stop the paint from dripping or how to balance bricks so that they will not fall down. • Introduce children to a wide range of music, painting and sculpture. • Encourage children to take time to think about painting or sculpture that is unfamiliar to them before they talk about it or express an opinion.
40-60+ months	• Begins to build a repertoire of songs and dances. • Explores the different sounds of instruments. • Explores what happens when they mix colours. • Experiments to create different textures. • Understands that different media can be combined to create new effects. • Manipulates materials to achieve a planned effect. • Constructs with a purpose in mind, using a variety of resources. • Uses simple tools and techniques competently and appropriately. • Selects appropriate resources and adapts work where necessary. • Selects tools and techniques needed to shape, assemble and join materials they are using. **Early Learning Goal** **Children sing songs, make music and dance, and experiment with ways of changing them. They safely use and explore a variety of materials, tools and techniques, experimenting with colour, design, texture, form and function.**	• Talk to children about ways of finding out what they can do with different media and what happens when they put different things together such as sand, paint and sawdust. • Encourage children to notice changes in properties of media as they are transformed through becoming wet, dry, flaky or fixed. Talk about what is happening, helping them to think about cause and effect.	• Provide resources for mixing colours, joining things together and combining materials, demonstrating where appropriate. • Provide children with opportunities to use their skills and explore concepts and ideas through their representations. • Have a 'holding bay' where models and works can be retained for a period for children to enjoy, develop, or refer to. • Plan imaginative, active experiences, such as 'Going on a bear hunt'. Help them remember the actions of the story (We're Going on a Bear Hunt by Michael Rosen and Helen Oxenbury) and think about the different ways of moving.

Children develop at their own rates, and in their own ways. The development statements and their order should not be taken as necessary steps for individual children. They should not be used as checklists. The age/stage bands overlap because these are not fixed age boundaries but suggest a typical range of development.

Playing and Exploring, Active Learning, and Creating and Thinking Critically support children's learning across all areas

Expressive Arts and Design: Being imaginative

	A Unique Child: observing what a child is learning	Positive Relationships: what adults could do	Enabling Environments: what adults could provide
Birth - 11 months	*Babies and toddlers need to explore the world and develop a range of ways to communicate before they can express their own ideas through arts and design.* See Characteristics of Effective Learning; Communication and Language; Physical Development; Personal, Social and Emotional Development	See Characteristics of Effective Learning; Communication and Language; Physical Development; Personal, Social and Emotional Development	See Characteristics of Effective Learning; Communication and Language; Physical Development; Personal, Social and Emotional Development
8-20 months	• Expresses self through physical action and sound. • Pretends that one object represents another, especially when objects have characteristics in common.	• Show genuine interest and be willing to play along with a young child who is beginning to pretend.	• Provide a variety of familiar resources reflecting everyday life, such as magazines, real kitchen items, telephones or washing materials.
16-26 months	• Beginning to use representation to communicate, e.g. drawing a line and saying 'That's me.' • Beginning to make-believe by pretending.	• Observe and encourage children's make-believe play in order to gain an understanding of their interests. • Sometimes speak quietly, slowly or gruffly for fun in pretend scenarios with children. • Be interested in the children's creative processes and talk to them about what they mean to them.	• Provide story boxes filled with interesting items to spark children's storytelling ideas. • Offer additional resources reflecting interests such as tunics, cloaks and bags.
22-36 months			

Children develop at their own rates, and in their own ways. The development statements and their order should not be taken as necessary steps for individual children. They should not be used as checklists. The age/stage bands overlap because these are not fixed age boundaries but suggest a typical range of development.

Playing and Exploring, Active Learning, and Creating and Thinking Critically support children's learning across all areas

Expressive arts and design: Being imaginative

	A Unique Child: observing what a child is learning	Positive Relationships: what adults could do	Enabling Environments: what adults could provide
30-50 months	• Developing preferences for forms of expression. • Uses movement to express feelings. • Creates movement in response to music. • Sings to self and makes up simple songs. • Makes up rhythms. • Notices what adults do, imitating what is observed and then doing it spontaneously when the adult is not there. • Engages in imaginative role-play based on own first-hand experiences. • Builds stories around toys, e.g. farm animals needing rescue from an armchair 'cliff'. • Uses available resources to create props to support role-play. • Captures experiences and responses with a range of media, such as music, dance and paint and other materials or words.	• Support children's excursions into imaginary worlds by encouraging inventiveness, offering support and advice on occasions and ensuring that they have experiences that stimulate their interest.	• Tell stories based on children's experiences and the people and places they know well. • Offer a story stimulus by suggesting an imaginary event or set of circumstances, e.g., "This bear has arrived in the post. He has a letter pinned to his jacket. It says 'Please look after this bear.' We should look after him in our room. How can we do that?."
40-60+ months	• Create simple representations of events, people and objects. • Initiates new combinations of movement and gesture in order to express and respond to feelings, ideas and experiences. • Chooses particular colours to use for a purpose. • Introduces a storyline or narrative into their play. • Plays alongside other children who are engaged in the same theme. • Plays cooperatively as part of a group to develop and act out a narrative. **Early Learning Goal** **Children use what they have learnt about media and materials in original ways, thinking about uses and purposes. They represent their own ideas, thoughts and feelings through design and technology, art, music, dance, role play and stories.**	• Help children to gain confidence in their own way of representing ideas. • Be aware of the link between imaginative play and children's ability to handle narrative. • Create imaginary words to describe, for example, monsters or other strong characters in stories and poems. • Carefully support children who are less confident. • Help children communicate through their bodies by encouraging expressive movement linked to their imaginative ideas. • Introduce descriptive language to support children, for example, 'rustle' and 'shuffle'.	• Extend children's experience and expand their imagination through the provision of pictures, paintings, poems, music, dance and story. • Provide a stimulus for imagination by introducing atmospheric features in the role play area, such as the sounds of rain beating on a roof, or placing a spotlight to suggest a stage set. Provide curtains and place dressing-up materials and instruments close by. • Make materials accessible so that children are able to imagine and develop their projects and ideas while they are still fresh in their minds and important to them. • Provide children with opportunities to use their skills and explore concepts and ideas through their representations. • Provide opportunities indoors and outdoors and support the different interests of children, e.g. in role-play of a builder's yard, encourage narratives to do with building and mending.

Children develop at their own rates, and in their own ways. The development statements and their order should not be taken as necessary steps for individual children.
They should not be used as checklists. The age/stage bands overlap because these are not fixed age boundaries but suggest a typical range of development